LAWS AND LEGISLATION

THE FOURTH AMENDMENT

IMPLICATIONS OF TECHNOLOGICAL SHIFTS AND SELECTED TRENDS

LAWS AND LEGISLATION

Additional books in this series can be found on Nova's website under the Series tab.

Additional e-books in this series can be found on Nova's website under the e-book tab.

LAWS AND LEGISLATION

THE FOURTH AMENDMENT

IMPLICATIONS OF TECHNOLOGICAL SHIFTS AND SELECTED TRENDS

LUCILLE E. HUFF
EDITOR

nova publishers
New York

For permission to use material from this book please contact us:
Telephone 631-231-7269; Fax 631-231-8175
Web Site: http://www.novapublishers.com

Additional color graphics may be available in the e-book version of this book.

Library of Congress Cataloging-in-Publication Data

ISBN: 978-1-63321-634-1

Published by Nova Science Publishers, Inc. † New York

CONTENTS

PREFACE

Chapter 1 – In the 1970s, the Supreme Court handed down *Smith v. Maryland* and *United States v. Miller*, two of the most important Fourth Amendment decisions of the 20th century. In these cases, the Court held that people are not entitled to an expectation of privacy in information they voluntarily provide to third parties. This legal proposition, known as the third-party doctrine, permits the government access to, as a matter of Fourth Amendment law, a vast amount of information about individuals, such as the websites they visit; who they have emailed; the phone numbers they dial; and their utility, banking, and education records, just to name a few. Questions have been raised whether this doctrine is still viable in light of the major technological and social changes over the past several decades.

Before there were emails, instant messaging, and other forms of electronic communication, it was much easier for the courts to determine if a government investigation constituted a Fourth Amendment "search." If the police intruded on your person, house, papers, or effects—tangible property interests listed in the text of the Fourth Amendment—that act was considered a search, which had to be "reasonable" under the circumstances. However, with the advent of intangible forms of communication, like the telephone or the Internet, it became much more difficult for judges to determine when certain surveillance practices intruded upon Fourth Amendment rights. With *Katz v. United States*, the Court supposedly remedied this by declaring that the Fourth Amendment protects not only a person's tangible things, but additionally, his right to privacy. *Katz*, however, left unprotected anything a person knowingly exposes to the public. This idea would form the basis of *Smith* and *Miller*. In those cases, the Court held that a customer has no reasonable expectation of privacy in the phone numbers he dials (*Smith*) and in checks and deposit slips he gives to his bank (*Miller*), as he has exposed them to another and assumed the risk they could be handed over to the government.

While the third-party doctrine has been criticized by Members of Congress, various commentators, and others as overly constrictive of Americans' privacy rights, it appears to fit relatively well with other Fourth Amendment case law. That being said, advancements in data collection, automation, and use have some questioning the continued application of this doctrine in a digital society. Several events have precipitated renewed debates over its continued existence. First was the Supreme Court's decision in the GPS tracking case, *United States v. Jones*, where two concurring opinions comprising five Justices of the Court called into question various existing Fourth Amendment theories, including the third-party doctrine, at least with respect to long-term government monitoring and advanced surveillance technology. Second was the Edward Snowden leaks relating to the National Security Agency's telephone metadata program, which has been primarily justified by *Smith* and the third-party doctrine. Various Members of Congress have joined the debate, with some introducing legislation that would require a warrant for access to records held by third-parties, and others introducing more targeted measures that would limit access to information such as geolocation data from third-party companies.

With these legal, social, and technological trends in mind, this report explores the third party-doctrine, including its historical background, its legal and practical underpinnings, and its present and potential future applications. It explores the major third-party doctrine cases and fits them within the larger Fourth Amendment framework. It surveys the various doctrinal and practical arguments for and against its continued application. Lastly, this report describes congressional efforts to supplement legal protection for access to third-party records, as well as suggesting possible future directions in the law.

Chapter 2 – Cloud computing is fast becoming an integral part of how we communicate with one another, buy music, share photos, conduct business, pay our bills, shop, and bank. Many of the activities that once occurred solely in the physical world, including communications with one another, are increasingly moving to the digital world. What was once a letter to a friend is now a Facebook message; a call to a loved one is now a Skype chat; a private meeting with a business partner is now a video conference call. In short, the cloud is revolutionizing not only how we compute, but also how we live. Where individuals once locked personal or business papers solely in a desk drawer or filing cabinet, they now also store them on someone else's computer.

In short, cloud computing is a web-based service that allows users to access anything from e-mail to social media on a third-party computer. For instance, Gmail and Yahoo are cloud-based email services that allow users to access and store emails that are saved on each respective service's computer, rather than on the individual's computer. As more communications are facilitated through these cloud-based programs, it is no surprise that government and law enforcement would seek to access this stored information to conduct criminal investigations, prevent cyber threats, and thwart terrorist attacks, among other purposes. This prompts the following questions: (1) What legal protections are in place for information shared and stored in the cloud? (2) What legal process must the government follow to obtain this information? and (3) How do these rules differ from those applied in the physical world?

Protections of communications in the physical world flow from the Fourth Amendment and various federal statutes such as the Electronic Communications Privacy Act of 1986 (ECPA), which includes the Stored Communications Act (SCA). Under the Fourth Amendment, government officials are generally prohibited from accessing an individual's communication, such as tapping into a telephone call or opening a postal letter, without first obtaining judicial approval. In the digital world, courts have by and large required law enforcement to acquire a warrant before accessing the contents of electronic communications, but have permitted law enforcement to access non-content information such as routing data with lesser process. These cases do not seem to distinguish between cloud-based and traditional forms of Internet services.

Federal courts have applied the SCA to various electronic communications including e-mails, messages sent on social networking sites like Facebook and MySpace, and movies posted on video-sharing sites like YouTube. The process for obtaining these communications under the SCA depends on how long the information has been stored with the service provider and how the provider is classified under the SCA. The relatively few cases dealing with cloud computing have required lesser legal process for accessing electronic communications sent via cloud-based services than traditional forms of Internet computing.

In light of this rapidly changing technology, there have been several legislative proposals to augment the Fourth Amendment's protections for digital communications and update existing statutory protections like the SCA for information shared and stored in the cloud.

Chapter 3 – Over the past few decades, state and federal lawmakers have promoted the development of databases containing DNA (deoxyribonucleic acid) profiles for individuals who are under the supervision of the criminal justice system due to their known or suspected involvement in a felony or other qualifying crime. Congress has demonstrated concern toward some aspects of DNA databanking by requiring expungement of a DNA profile in certain circumstances, prohibiting most non-forensic uses of DNA profiles and databases, and restricting familial searching. However, in general, Congress has taken a supportive attitude toward DNA databanking and has incentivized the development, expansion, and integration of DNA databases.

As DNA database programs have widened in scope and grown in numbers, their consistency with the Fourth Amendment's prohibition on unreasonable searches and seizures has increasingly been challenged. In the context of compulsory DNA collection, courts have widely upheld laws mandating the collection of DNA from persons who were convicted and are subject to the penal system's custody or supervision. Far fewer cases have addressed whether DNA collection from arrestees is also constitutional. The two federal circuit courts of appeals to hear the question upheld the mandatory DNA profiling of *indicted* arrestees, but no federal court has assessed the constitutionality of profiling arrestees in the absence of a judicial finding of probable cause.

Courts have generally upheld the use and permanent storage of a lawfully databanked DNA profile. However, not all courts agree that *any* post-conviction use of those profiles is constitutionally acceptable. In particular, observers are now raising questions about the Fourth Amendment consistency of using databases for non-forensic purposes and for familial searching—that is, using the DNA databases to locate potential relatives of an unidentified suspect. Currently, these concerns are largely confined to the scholarly literature—they have not come before a federal court—and are primarily centered on state database programs. Unlike some state DNA databases, the National DNA Index System (NDIS) and the Combined DNA Index System (CODIS) can not be used for either non-forensic research or intentional familial searching. However, the increase in states that authorize familial searching suggests that it may not be long before the constitutionality of familial searching comes before a federal court.

As these issues percolate up to the courts, new advances and revelations in the science of forensic analysis and databanking may have potentially significant legal implications. Several courts have suggested that new forensic techniques and scientific findings would require them to reevaluate their legal conclusions and analysis. In particular, research into the scope and nature of the information revealed by the "junk" DNA used in forensic analysis may alter how courts measure the intrusiveness of DNA profiling if it suggests that "junk" DNA reveals more sensitive information about its source than scientists previously thought.

Chapter 4 – As technology continues to advance, what was once thought novel, even a luxury, quickly becomes commonplace, even a necessity. Global Positioning System (GPS) technology is one such example. Generally, GPS is a satellite-based technology that discloses the location of a given object. This technology is used in automobiles and cell phones to provide individual drivers with directional assistance. Just as individuals are finding increasing applications for GPS technology, state and federal governments are as well. State and federal law enforcement use various forms of GPS technology to obtain evidence in criminal investigations. For example, federal prosecutors have used information from cellular phone service providers that allows real-time tracking of the locations of customers' cellular phones. Title III of the Omnibus Crime Control and Safe Streets Act of 1958 (P.L. 90-351) regulates the interception of wire, oral, and electronic communications. As such, it does not regulate the use of GPS technology affixed to vehicles and is beyond the scope of this report. However, bills introduced in the 112th Congress, such as S. 1212 and H.R. 2168, would address circumstances under which law enforcement may obtain, use, or disclose GPS data.

The increased reliance on GPS technology raises important societal and legal considerations. Some contend that law enforcement's use of such technology to track motor vehicles' movements provides for a safer society. Conversely, others have voiced concerns that GPS technology could be used to reveal information inherently private. Defendants on both the state and federal levels are raising Fourth Amendment constitutional challenges, asking the courts to require law enforcement to first obtain a warrant before using GPS technology.

Subject to a few exceptions, the Fourth Amendment of the U.S. Constitution requires law enforcement to obtain a warrant before conducting a search or making a seizure. Courts continue to grapple with the specific issue of whether law enforcement's use of GPS technology constitutes a search or seizure, as well as the broader question of how the Constitution should address advancing technology in general. The Supreme Court may provide some answers in *United States v. Jones* (131 S.Ct. 3064 (2011)) when it addresses the issue of whether law enforcement's use of GPS technology in connection with motor vehicles falls within the Fourth Amendment's purview. Lower federal courts have arrived at varying conclusions. Several district and circuit courts of appeals have concluded that law enforcement's current use of GPS technology does not constitute a search, and is thus permissible, under the Constitution. One circuit court has found the duration of GPS tracking to be constitutionally significant. State legislatures and state courts have approached the issue in various ways. Some states have enacted laws requiring law enforcement to obtain a warrant before using GPS technology. Some state courts have resolved the question under their own constitutions. Other state courts have relied on Supreme Court precedent, such as *United States v. Knotts*, 460 U.S. 276 (1983), to derive an answer.

This report discusses the basics of GPS technology, society's reliance on it, and some of the related legal and privacy implications. In addition, the report examines legislative and judicial responses on both federal and state levels.

Chapter 5 – The prospect of drone use inside the United States raises far-reaching issues concerning the extent of government surveillance authority, the value of privacy in the digital age, and the role of Congress in reconciling these issues.

Drones, or unmanned aerial vehicles (UAVs), are aircraft that can fly without an onboard human operator. An unmanned aircraft system (UAS) is the entire system, including the aircraft, digital network, and personnel on the ground. Drones can fly either by remote control or on a predetermined flight path; can be as small as an insect and as large as a traditional jet; can be produced more cheaply than traditional aircraft; and can keep operators out of harm's way. These unmanned aircraft are most commonly known for their operations overseas in tracking down and killing suspected members of Al Qaeda and related organizations. In addition to these missions abroad, drones are being considered for use in domestic surveillance operations to protect the homeland, assist in crime fighting, disaster relief, immigration control, and environmental monitoring.

Although relatively few drones are currently flown over U.S. soil, the Federal Aviation Administration (FAA) predicts that 30,000 drones will fill the nation's skies in less than 20 years. Congress has played a large role in this expansion. In February 2012, Congress enacted the FAA Modernization and Reform Act (P.L. 112-95), which calls for the FAA to accelerate the integration of unmanned aircraft into the national airspace system by 2015. However, some Members of Congress and the public fear there are insufficient safeguards in place to ensure that drones are not used to spy on American citizens and unduly infringe upon their fundamental privacy. These observers caution that the FAA is primarily charged with ensuring air traffic safety, and is not adequately prepared to handle the issues of privacy and civil liberties raised by drone use.

This report assesses the use of drones under the Fourth Amendment right to be free from unreasonable searches and seizures. The touchstone of the Fourth Amendment is reasonableness. A reviewing court's determination of the reasonableness of a drone search would likely be informed by location of the search, the sophistication of the technology used, and society's conception of privacy in an age of rapid technological advancement. While individuals can expect substantial protections against warrantless government intrusions into their homes, the Fourth Amendment offers less robust restrictions upon government surveillance occurring in public places including areas immediately outside the home, such as in driveways or backyards. Concomitantly, as technology advances, the contours of what is reasonable under the Fourth Amendment may adjust as people's expectations of privacy evolve.

In the 113th Congress, several measures have been introduced that would restrict the use of drones at home. Several of the bills would require law enforcement to obtain a warrant before using drones for domestic surveillance, subject to several exceptions. Others would establish a regime under which the drone user must file a data collection statement stating when, where, how the drone will be used and how the user will minimize the collection of information protected by the legislation.

In: The Fourth Amendment
Editor: Lucille E. Huff
ISBN: 978-1-63321-634-1

Chapter 1

THE FOURTH AMENDMENT THIRD-PARTY DOCTRINE*

Richard M. Thompson II

SUMMARY

In the 1970s, the Supreme Court handed down *Smith v. Maryland* and *United States v. Miller*, two of the most important Fourth Amendment decisions of the 20th century. In these cases, the Court held that people are not entitled to an expectation of privacy in information they voluntarily provide to third parties. This legal proposition, known as the third-party doctrine, permits the government access to, as a matter of Fourth Amendment law, a vast amount of information about individuals, such as the websites they visit; who they have emailed; the phone numbers they dial; and their utility, banking, and education records, just to name a few. Questions have been raised whether this doctrine is still viable in light of the major technological and social changes over the past several decades.

Before there were emails, instant messaging, and other forms of electronic communication, it was much easier for the courts to determine if a government investigation constituted a Fourth Amendment "search." If the police intruded on your person, house, papers, or effects—tangible property interests listed in the text of the Fourth Amendment—that act

* This is an edited, reformatted and augmented version of a Congressional Research Service publication, No. R43586, dated June 5, 2014.

was considered a search, which had to be "reasonable" under the circumstances. However, with the advent of intangible forms of communication, like the telephone or the Internet, it became much more difficult for judges to determine when certain surveillance practices intruded upon Fourth Amendment rights. With *Katz v. United States*, the Court supposedly remedied this by declaring that the Fourth Amendment protects not only a person's tangible things, but additionally, his right to privacy. *Katz*, however, left unprotected anything a person knowingly exposes to the public. This idea would form the basis of *Smith* and *Miller*. In those cases, the Court held that a customer has no reasonable expectation of privacy in the phone numbers he dials (*Smith*) and in checks and deposit slips he gives to his bank (*Miller*), as he has exposed them to another and assumed the risk they could be handed over to the government.

While the third-party doctrine has been criticized by Members of Congress, various commentators, and others as overly constrictive of Americans' privacy rights, it appears to fit relatively well with other Fourth Amendment case law. That being said, advancements in data collection, automation, and use have some questioning the continued application of this doctrine in a digital society. Several events have precipitated renewed debates over its continued existence. First was the Supreme Court's decision in the GPS tracking case, *United States v. Jones*, where two concurring opinions comprising five Justices of the Court called into question various existing Fourth Amendment theories, including the third-party doctrine, at least with respect to long-term government monitoring and advanced surveillance technology. Second was the Edward Snowden leaks relating to the National Security Agency's telephone metadata program, which has been primarily justified by *Smith* and the third-party doctrine. Various Members of Congress have joined the debate, with some introducing legislation that would require a warrant for access to records held by third-parties, and others introducing more targeted measures that would limit access to information such as geolocation data from third-party companies.

With these legal, social, and technological trends in mind, this report explores the third party-doctrine, including its historical background, its legal and practical underpinnings, and its present and potential future applications. It explores the major third-party doctrine cases and fits them within the larger Fourth Amendment framework. It surveys the various doctrinal and practical arguments for and against its continued application. Lastly, this report describes congressional efforts to supplement legal protection for access to third-party records, as well as suggesting possible future directions in the law.

INTRODUCTION

In 1967, the Supreme Court pronounced in *Katz v. United States* that "[w]hat a person knowingly exposes to the public, even in his own home or office, is not a subject of Fourth Amendment protection."[1] This rule "that a person has no legitimate expectation of privacy in information he voluntarily turns over to third parties" is known as the "third-party doctrine."[2] While its reach in the pre-digital age was relatively limited, the third-party doctrine has provided the government a powerful investigative tool in a society where people share ever-increasing amounts of information with others. Many have debated whether these technological and social changes require the courts to reconsider this doctrine, or, alternatively, whether Congress should step in and create some form of statutory protection for this information.[3]

Over the years, the Court has applied the third-party doctrine to two main sets of cases. In one, the Court has held that people do not have a reasonable expectation that a person with whom they are communicating will not later reveal that conversation to the police.[4] In the second, the Court extended this doctrine to hold that people are not entitled to Fourth Amendment safeguards for records given to a third-party or data generated as part of a person's business transactions with a third-party. In two of the most prominent third-party cases, *Smith v. Maryland* and *United States v. Miller*, the Court held that government access to telephone calling records and bank records, respectively, were not Fourth Amendment searches for which warrants were required.[5]

To be clear, the third-party doctrine does not cover all conceivable information that is transferred through a third party. For instance, the content of a voice or email communication does not fall within its scope.[6] The courts have reasoned that the service provider is merely the conduit or intermediary of those communications and not the recipient; thus, the user does not lose privacy protection in those communications. On the other hand, both non-content and content information that is shared directly with a service provider is covered by the third-party doctrine (e.g., the deposit slips or checks shared with a bank and data kept by the bank relating to transactions with it). Additionally, non-content information derived from private interactions with others is subject to the third-party doctrine. This covers data such as telephone numbers dialed, email addresses of those emailed, or websites visited.

The third-party doctrine has been heavily criticized for unnecessarily constricting Americans' privacy rights.[7] But whatever one thinks of the rule that citizens are not entitled to Fourth Amendment protection when they share information with one another, the third-party doctrine is largely entrenched in other areas of Fourth Amendment case law. For example, it is not a Fourth Amendment search for the police to dig through one's trash left on the curb,[8] to track a person's movements on public streets,[9] and even to surveil a person in a fenced-in backyard with an aircraft.[10] In each of these instances, the Court reasoned that because the person exposed his activities to the public gaze he was no longer entitled to an expectation of privacy.

In addition to the legal attacks on the third-party doctrine, some have questioned its practical implications in a society which shares almost every facet of its life with various entities.[11] Both *Smith* and *Miller*, decided in the mid- to late-1970s, came before the mass digital revolution experienced over the last several decades. Since these decisions, there has been a wave of advancement in data generation, collection, automation, and processing.[12] Whether these new technologies and shifts in social interaction require courts or lawmakers to revise this review is currently under debate.

Two major events in the past few years typify this ongoing debate. The first is the conversation prompted by several concurrences in the 2012 GPS tracking case *United States v. Jones*.[13] In two concurring opinions in that case, five Justices opined that warrantless, pervasive government location monitoring can violate the Fourth Amendment.[14] Commentators have speculated that these five votes could have significant consequences for other similar ubiquitous surveillance techniques.[15] And at least one member of the Court, Justice Sotomayor, believes that the third-party doctrine should be seriously rethought as a whole. The second is the litigation surrounding the National Security Agency's telephone metadata program. Several federal courts, including the Foreign Intelligence Surveillance Court, have applied *Smith* and the third-party doctrine to uphold this comprehensive data collection program.[16] One district court judge, however, found *Smith* outdated and the NSA program too invasive for *Smith* to still control this legal question.[17]

With these shifts in technology and legal thinking in mind, this report explores the history and legal foundations of the third-party doctrine. It will first provide background to the Fourth Amendment and describe in what instances government investigations trigger its protections. It will then analyze the Court's third-party doctrine cases and provide doctrinal and practical arguments for and against its application. Next, this report will examine how Congress has responded to the third-party doctrine and whether *United States v. Jones* and subsequent cases might alter its future application. Lastly, this report will consider any potential future developments in this fast-moving area of law.

FOURTH AMENDMENT BACKGROUND

Before the advent of modern communications, government officials could not simply subpoena an Internet Service Provider (ISP), or Amazon, or Google for information relating to a target of investigation, but had to enter the suspect's home or office, sometimes by force, to retrieve personal information directly themselves.[18] During the 18th century, British and colonial officials conducted searches and seizures of people's homes with little to no suspicion of wrongdoing pursuant to either a general warrant, which was used mainly in England, or a writ of assistance, which was used in the American colonies.[19] These indiscriminate government intrusions contributed to the people's fear of unrestrained government power and led to the eventual passage of the Fourth Amendment.

Take, for instance, the formative English search and seizure case *Entick v. Carrington*, where the government was investigating John Entick and others for alleged publication of seditious articles.[20] In that case, government officials broke into Entick's home with "force and arms," pried open the locks on his doors, broke open his chests and drawers, and searched his private papers and books for four hours.[21] The officers conducted this search under the guise of a general warrant, a legal order which states with a high level of generality the places and things to be searched and seized. In outlawing these practices, Lord Camden of the English bench observed:

> [O]ur law holds the property of every man so sacred, that no man can set his foot upon his neighbour's close without his leave; if he does he is a trespasser, though he does no damage at all; if he will tread upon his neighbour's ground, he must justify it by law.[22]

These same intrusive practices also faced disfavor in the American colonies. British officials often resorted to writs of assistance, a form of general warrant, which permitted house-to-house searches.[23] These legal orders generally failed to allege any illegal activity and were not signed off on by a judge.[24] In the famous *Paxton's Case*, leading Boston attorney James Otis attacked these writs as "the worst instrument of arbitrary power, the most destructive of English liberty, and the fundamental principles of the constitution, that was ever found in an English law book."[25] John Adams later commented that these indiscriminate intrusions were "the spark in which originated the American Revolution."[26]

To prevent the newly established federal government from committing these incursions into their lives, the American people ratified the Fourth Amendment as part of the Bill of Rights in 1791. It reads:

> The right of the people to be secure in their persons, houses, papers, and effects, against unreasonable searches and seizures, shall not be violated, and no Warrants shall issue, but upon probable cause, supported by Oath of affirmation, and particularly describing the place to be searched, and the person or things to be seized.[27]

Over the years, the federal courts have struggled to reconcile the first clause of the Amendment, which requires that all searches and seizures be reasonable, with the second clause, which requires that all warrants meet certain minimum requirements such as particularly describing the place to be searched and the things to be seized.[28] In any event, the Court must first determine whether the Fourth Amendment's restrictions apply at all. This is done by asking whether the government has conducted a "search," a legal term of art that cannot be resolved by mere dictionary definition, but instead requires application of the Supreme Court's intricate, and at times contradictory, Fourth Amendment case law.

Early Definitions of a Fourth Amendment "Search"

Although the Fourth Amendment was ratified in 1791, the Supreme Court's first in-depth interpretation of what constitutes a Fourth Amendment search did not arise until the 1886 case *United States v. Boyd.*[29] In *Boyd*, the government obtained a court order for the Boyds to provide an invoice of goods they imported which the government planned to use against them in court. The Boyds produced the invoice, but protested that its production constituted an unreasonable search and seizure under the Fourth Amendment. Looking to *Entick* and other pre-Revolutionary cases for guidance, the Court found that the production of private papers was so similar to an actual invasion into one's home that it constituted a Fourth Amendment search.[30]

Although *Boyd* instructed that the Fourth Amendment should be "liberally construed,"[31] the Court narrowed the scope of what constitutes a search in *Olmstead v. United States.*[32] In that case, federal agents investigating the bootlegging activities of a criminal syndicate placed a wiretap on several phone lines running from the homes and office of four suspects. At no point did the officers trespass upon the defendants' property to conduct the tap. The Court held that these wiretaps should not be considered a search as the "Amendment itself shows that the search is to be of material things—the person, house, papers, and effects," and the intangible voice of the defendants was not covered by its literal terms. The Court further found that the agents did not engage in "an actual physical invasion" of Olmstead's home for purposes of conducting the wiretap.[33] Dissenting in *Olmstead*, Justice Brandeis observed that in the past, most notably in *Boyd*, the Court "refused to place an unduly literal construction" upon the Fourth Amendment.[34] Instead, he continued:

> The protection guaranteed by the amendment[] is much broader in scope. The makers of our Constitution ... sought to protect Americans in their beliefs, their thoughts, their emotions and their sensations. They conferred, as against the government, the right to be let alone-the most comprehensive of rights and the right most valued by civilized men. To protect, that right, every unjustifiable intrusion by the government upon the privacy of the individual, whatever the means employed, must be deemed a violation of the Fourth Amendment.[35]

Nonetheless, in the ensuing years, the Court assessed whether there was a search based on whether a physical trespass occurred. For instance, it was not considered a search when police engaged in eavesdropping absent a trespass.[36] However, where the police trespassed upon the suspect's property—even by an inch—the Court held that the Fourth Amendment applied.[37] Forty years later the Court would expressly overrule *Olmstead*'s literal, trespass-based interpretation of the Fourth Amendment for a privacy-based test.

Reasonable Expectation of Privacy and the Secrecy Model of Privacy

In 1967, the Court decided *Katz v. United States*, which abandoned the literal interpretation of the Fourth Amendment—one that protected only persons, houses, papers, and effects—to one that also protected intangible interests such as privacy.[38] However, while the Court sought to expand what the Fourth Amendment protects, certain passages in *Katz* simultaneously foreclosed protection for anything a person exposes to the public or another person. This would have significant consequences for government access to records and other information held by third parties.

In *Katz*, the FBI was investigating the illegal gambling activities of Mr. Katz. The FBI had attached an electronic eavesdropping device to the outside of the telephone booth in which Katz made calls and offered evidence of these calls against Katz at his prosecution. Quite sensibly, the parties framed the question presented in light of *Olmstead*'s physical trespass theory, the controlling Fourth Amendment theory of the day. They debated whether a telephone booth was a "constitutionally protected area" such that attaching the listening device to its outside would constitute a Fourth Amendment search.[39] The Court, speaking through Justice Stewart, looked beyond this traditional inquiry into protected areas, and instead declared that the "Fourth Amendment protects people, not places."[40] He observed that the "Amendment protects individual privacy against certain kinds of governmental intrusion," but also instructed that it "cannot be translated into a general constitutional 'right to privacy[.]'" Such a "right to be let alone by other people" is left largely to protection under state law.[41] In bypassing *Olmstead* and formulating the scope of the Fourth Amendment in light of privacy principles, it became necessary for the Court to lay down a rule to determine which privacy interests would be protected and which would not. Unfortunately, the majority provided little by way of guidance on the scope of this rule, beyond to say that what a person "seeks to preserve as private, even in an area accessible to the public, may be constitutionally protected" and that the use of the electronic eavesdropping device violated Katz's privacy, upon which he "justifiably relied."[42] Concurring, Justice Harlan developed a two-part framework for answering this question, which would become *Katz*'s controlling test.[43] Under Justice Harlan's formulation, a court first asks whether the person exhibited an actual or subjective expectation of privacy and second whether society is likely to deem that expectation reasonable.[44]

Beyond its general assertion that the Fourth Amendment protects people, not places, the majority made an equally far-reaching observation that "[w]hat a person knowingly exposes to the public, even in his own home or office, is not a subject of Fourth Amendment protection."[45] This rule adopts what can be called the secrecy model of privacy. Under the secrecy model, once a fact is disclosed to the public in any way, the information is no longer entitled to privacy protection.[46] This secrecy model, along with the assumption of the risk theory discussed below, would form the underpinnings of the modern third-party doctrine.

THIRD-PARTY DOCTRINE JURISPRUDENCE

The idea that what a person knowingly exposes to the public is not entitled to constitutional protection was not an invention of the *Katz* court, but was embedded in Fourth Amendment jurisprudence for quite some time. In one of the first Fourth Amendment cases, *Ex parte Jackson*, the Court held that anything "exposed" on the outside of a parcel of mail is not entitled to Fourth Amendment protection.[47] Similarly, under what has come to be known as the "plain view" doctrine, Justice Brandeis noted in the 1927 case *United States v. Lee* that the use of a searchlight to view cases of liquor on the deck of a ship was not a Fourth Amendment search.[48] More prominently, the Court decided a series of cases throughout the 20th century holding that people do not have a reasonable expectation that a person with whom they are conversing will not later reveal that conversation to the police. The third-party doctrine would later be extended to documents and transactional data shared with third parties.

Undercover Informant Cases

In a series of five cases throughout the 20th century, the Supreme Court assessed the constitutionality of the use of undercover agents or informants under the Fourth Amendment. In *On Lee v. United States*, the government wired an "undercover agent" with a microphone and sent him into On Lee's laundromat to engage him in incriminating conversation.[49] An agent of the Bureau of Narcotics sat outside with a receiving set to hear the conversation. In the course of these conversations, On Lee made incriminating statements, which the agent later testified to at On Lee's trial. On Lee argued that this evidence was obtained in violation of the Fourth Amendment. In an opinion authored by Justice Jackson, the Court disagreed, noting that On Lee was "talking confidentially and indiscreetly with one he trusted" and that the agent was let into his shop "with the consent, if not implied invitation" of On Lee.[50]

In a similar case, *Lopez v. United States*, the defendant attempted to bribe an internal revenue agent, who during some of these conversations was wearing a recording device.[51] At trial, Lopez moved to suppress evidence of the wire recordings as fruits of an unlawful search. Relying on the *On Lee* decision, the Court rejected this argument on the grounds that the defendant consented to the agent being in his office and "knew full well" that the statements he made to the agent could be used against him.[52] Further, the Court noted that the listening device was not used to intercept conversations the agent could not have otherwise heard, but "instead, the device was used only to obtain the most reliable evidence possible of a conversation in which the Government's own agent was a participant and which that agent was fully entitled to disclose."[53]

In *Lewis v. United States*, the government sent an undercover federal narcotics agent to the defendant's home several times to purchase marijuana.[54] Over the defendant's objections, the agent was permitted to recount the conversations at trial. Upon review, the Supreme Court held that the conversations were not protected under the Fourth Amendment as the defendant had invited the federal agent into his home and that the statements were "willingly" made to the agent.[55]

Finally, in *Hoffa v. United States*, a government informant relayed to federal law enforcement agents the many conversations he had with Jimmy Hoffa about Hoffa's attempt to tamper with a jury.[56] Because the informant did not enter Hoffa's hotel room by force, was invited to participate in the conversations by Hoffa, and was not a "surreptitious eavesdropper," the Court concluded that the Fourth Amendment had not been violated.[57]

There appear to be two motivating principles underlying these undercover informant cases. In one sense, the Court was applying *Olmstead*'s physical invasion test: because the informants had not trespassed into the defendants' homes or offices—in the words of pre-*Katz* case law, their "constitutionally protected areas"—there could be no constitutional invasion.[58] Rather, in each instance, the informant was invited onto the premises. For example, in *On Lee*, the Court observed that On Lee could not raise the issue of trespass as he had consented, if not invited, the agent to enter his business. A claim of trespass could only be made if the agent had entered by force or by show of authority.[59] In another sense, the Court found that voluntarily telling another person something gave him consent to share that information with another person including the government.[60] For instance, *Hoffa* instructed that the Fourth Amendment does not protect "a wrongdoer's misplaced belief that a person to whom he voluntarily confides his wrongdoing will not reveal it."[61]

Note that these cases came before *Katz* shifted the Fourth Amendment focus from property to privacy. Whether *Katz* would disturb this line of cases was a matter of "considerable speculation"[62] until the Court decided *United States v. White* four years later. In *White*, an undercover informant wearing a radio transmitter engaged the defendant in several incriminating conversations, four of which took place at the informant's house, and several other conversations took place in the defendant's home, a restaurant, and in the informant's car.[63] The court of appeals in *White* interpreted *Katz* as implicitly overruling this line of cases as it was based on a trespass doctrine that was "squarely discarded" in *Katz*.[64] The Supreme Court disagreed, however, and upheld the surreptitious surveillance. The opinion accepted that the trespass rationale could not survive after *Katz*, but that the undercover informant cases were also supported by a "second and independent ground"—that the informant was not an uninvited eavesdropper, but a party to the conversation who was free to report what he heard to the authorities.[65] For the Court, White had assumed the risk that information he shared with the informant could be shared with the police.[66]

With *White*, the Court combined several ideas in its Fourth Amendment jurisprudence: first, that it is unreasonable for people to expect privacy in information they share with another, and second, that they assume the risk that that information can be handed over to the government.[67] With these two theories in mind, the Court resolved two major third-party doctrine cases in the 1970s, *United States v. Miller* and *Smith v. Maryland*.[68] These cases would become the cornerstone of the modern third-party doctrine, and have been heavily relied upon by government officials to access various types of transactional data without a search warrant.

Miller v. United States—Subpoena for Bank Records

In 1976, the Court took up its first major third-party doctrine case to deal with transactional documents in *Miller v. United States*. In that case, agents of the Treasury Department's Alcohol, Tobacco, and Firearms Bureau were investigating Mitch Miller for his participation in an illegal whiskey distillery.[69] The agents subpoenaed the presidents of several banks in which Miller had an account to produce all records of accounts including savings, checking accounts, and any loans he may have had. The banks never informed Miller that the subpoenas had been served, but ordered their employees to comply with the subpoenas. At one bank, an agent was shown microfilm of Miller's account and provided copies of "one deposit slip and one or two checks."[70] At the other bank, the agent was shown similar records and was given copies of "all checks, deposit slips, two financial statements, and three monthly statements."[71] Copies of the checks were later introduced into evidence at Miller's trial.

The lower court held that the government had unlawfully circumvented the Fourth Amendment by first requiring the banks to maintain the customer's records for a certain period of time and second by using insufficient legal process to obtain those records from the bank. In a 7-2 ruling, the Supreme Court reversed and held that subpoenaing the bank records without a warrant did not violate the Fourth Amendment. The opinion by Justice Powell discarded the first argument by noting that previous case law held that merely requiring the bank to retain its customers' records did not constitute a Fourth Amendment search.[72] That previous case, however, did not resolve whether a subpoena was sufficient to access those documents.[73] Miller argued that the bank kept copies of personal records that he gave to the bank for a limited purpose and in which he retained a reasonable expectation of privacy under *Katz*. The Court, applying language from *Katz*, noted that "[w]hat a person knowingly exposes to the public ... is not a subject of Fourth Amendment protection."[74] The Court concluded that banking documents were not "confidential communications," but rather negotiable instruments that were required to transact business between the customer and the bank. All of the documents contained information "voluntarily conveyed to the banks and exposed to their employees in the ordinary course of business."[75] As with the undercover agent cases, once documents were shared with the bank, they could then be given to the government without requiring a search warrant. Citing to *White*, Justice Powell instructed that a bank customer "takes the risk, in revealing his affairs to another, that the information will be conveyed by that person to the government."[76] Looking to both this assumption of the risk theory and the secrecy model, the Court then included the following sentence which would come to encapsulate the third-party doctrine:

> This Court has held repeatedly that the Fourth Amendment does not prohibit the obtaining of information revealed to a third party and conveyed by him to Government authorities, even if the information is revealed on the assumption that it will be used only for a limited purpose and the confidence placed in the third party will not be betrayed.[77]

Based on this assertion, Miller could have no reasonable expectation of privacy in the bank records and thus the introduction of them at his prosecution did not contravene the Fourth Amendment.

Smith v. Maryland—Subpoena for Telephone Call Records

Several years later, the Court took up the second major third-party doctrine case, *Smith v. Maryland,*[78] which would have major implications for government collection of transactional records, especially those held by third-party companies.

In *Smith*, the police were investigating the robbery of a young woman, who gave the police a description of her assailant and the vehicle seen near the scene of the crime.[79] The police later spotted a man matching the victim's description driving an identical vehicle in her neighborhood, which they traced back to Michael Smith. Upon police request, the telephone company installed a pen register at its central office to record the telephone numbers dialed from Smith's home. The device was installed without a warrant or court order. Through the pen register, the police learned that a call was placed from Smith's home to the victim's phone, which would eventually connect Smith to the robbery. At trial, Smith claimed that any evidence obtained from the pen register violated his Fourth Amendment rights as the police failed to obtain a warrant before installing it. This motion was denied, Smith was later convicted of robbery, and the appeals court affirmed his conviction, holding that the installation of the pen register was not a Fourth Amendment search.[80]

In line with Justice Harlan's formulation of the *Katz* privacy test, the Supreme Court asked the following questions: first, whether Smith had a subjective expectation of privacy in the numbers he dialed, and second, whether that expectation was reasonable.[81] As to the former, the Court "doubt[ed] that people in general entertain any actual expectation of privacy in the numbers they dial."[82] The Court assumed that people, in the main, know and understand that they must convey the dialed numbers to the company to complete the call; that the company has a process of recording those numbers; and that the company actually does record those numbers for various business reasons. It deduced this partially from the fact that phone books inform consumers that the telephone companies "can frequently help in identifying to authorities the origin of unwelcome and untroublesome calls" and that customers see a list of their calls recorded on their monthly phone bills.[83]

Even if *Smith* did harbor a subjective expectation of privacy, the Court found that "this expectation is not 'one society is prepared to recognize as 'reasonable.''"[84] Justice Blackmun cited to *Miller*, *White*, *Hoffa*, and *Lopez* for the proposition that "a person has no legitimate expectation of privacy in information that he voluntarily turns over to third parties."[85] Because Smith "voluntarily conveyed" the telephone numbers to the company in the process of making the call, he had "exposed" that information to the company's equipment in the "ordinary course of business" and thus could not reasonably expect privacy in that information.[86] Moreover, the Court found that Smith "assumed the risk" that the telephone company would reveal to the police the numbers he dialed.[87]

Although *Smith* was the Court's last significant pronouncement on the parameters of the third-party doctrine, the lower federal courts have applied it in various contexts, with a significant number of these cases dealing with the transfer of electronic information.

Other Applications of the Third-Party Doctrine

After *Miller* and *Smith*, the courts have applied the third-party doctrine to a host of various scenarios including metadata connected to Internet communications, cell phone location information, and utility billing records, among others. These cases generally divide along a content/non-content distinction: the content of a communication, such as the body of an email, does not fall within third-party doctrine, and other Fourth Amendment rules apply. Addressing information, such as the to/from line in an email, the outside of a letter, or the telephone numbers dialed, however, are covered by the doctrine. There have been various rationales for this divide, the most compelling being the difference between the recipient of the information and companies that act merely as a conduit or intermediary between two people communicating with each other.

The difference in constitutional treatment between the content of a communication and its non-content addressing information dates at least as far back as the 19th century. In the 1877 case *Ex parte Jackson*, the Supreme Court held that the content of a mailed letter was protected under the Fourth Amendment, while the information exposed to the public, such as the address written on the outside, was not.[88] This dichotomy was further developed in *Katz* and *Smith*. In *Katz*, the Court protected the content of Mr. Katz's communication (his voice), noting that a caller is "surely entitled to assume that the words he utters into the mouthpiece will not be broadcast to the world."[89] *Non*-content information was not before the Court in *Katz*. On the other hand, *Smith* left non-content information, the numbers he dialed, unprotected, as pen registers do not allow law enforcement to "hear sound" and "[n]either the purport of any communication between the caller and the recipient of the call, their identities, nor whether the call was even completed is disclosed[.]"[90]

This distinction between content and non-content has also been applied in the lower courts. In *United States v. Warshak*, the Sixth Circuit Court of Appeals held that individuals enjoy a reasonable expectation of privacy in the *content* of their emails.[91] The panel noted that "email requires strong protection under the Fourth Amendment; otherwise, the Fourth Amendment would prove an ineffective guardian of private communication, an essential purpose it has long been recognized to serve."[92] Following *Smith*'s lead, the courts have taken the opposite approach to non-content or addressing information that accompanies an email or other electronic communications. In *United States v. Forrester*, for example, the Ninth Circuit Court of Appeals held that the to/from addresses of emails, the IP addresses of websites a person visits, and the total volume of data transmitted to or from a certain account were not subject to Fourth Amendment protection.[93] The Ninth Circuit found that like the telephone numbers in *Smith*, email and Internet users should know that addressing information "is provided to and used by Internet Service Providers (ISP) for the specific purpose of directing the routing of information."[94] Moreover, the court noted that although the government can make an "educated guess" about what was said in a message or viewed on a particular website, this information does not "necessarily reveal any more about the underlying contents of the communication than do phone numbers."[95] Further emphasizing this distinction, while *Smith* covered the telephone numbers a person dials to make a call, government access to the numbers dialed after a call has been placed, known as "post-cut through dialed digits," is considered a Fourth Amendment search.[96] These numbers, which might include "bank account numbers, Social Security numbers, prescription numbers, and the like," constitute the "contents of communications" and are "the kind of information that an individual wants and reasonably expects to be kept private."[97]

Another dividing line between protected and unprotected information pertains to the identity of the service provider in the chain of communication. If the provider is seen as a party to the transaction and is a *recipient* of the information, the records are generally considered "business records" of that company and subject to the third-party doctrine. This rationale is similar to that applied in the undercover informant cases. Although the information provided to an informant constitutes the content of the communication, it is not protected because it was spoken directly to the agent—in other words, the agent was the *recipient* of that information. Alternatively, where the company merely acts as a *conduit* or *intermediary* and "passively convey[s]" that information to an end-user, the material is generally not subject to the third-party doctrine.[98]

In *Warshak*, the Sixth Circuit noted that the ISP was acting as an "intermediary that makes email communication possible."[99] Just like the post office which acts as an intermediary of a letter, and the telephone company which acts as an intermediary to the voice content of phone calls, "emails must pass through an ISP's server to reach their intended recipient."[100] And just as the police are prohibited from accessing communications from the post office or a telephone company without first obtaining a warrant, the Sixth Circuit held that a warrant should equally be required to access more modern forms of communications.[101] Distinguishing the bank records case *Miller*, the court found that whereas the bank records, checks, and deposit slips in *Miller* were given directly to the banks to be used in the "ordinary course of business," the ISP was the "intermediary, not the intended recipient of the emails."[102] The court rejected the government's arguments that the "ability" and "right" of the ISP to access emails stored on its servers should eliminate any Fourth Amendment privacy interests, as a similar ability of the telephone operators in *Katz* to listen in on conversations carried over their system did not eliminate a user's reasonable expectation of privacy.[103]

Another prominent example of this conduit versus recipient dichotomy can be found in lower federal court cases treating cell location data as a business record not subject to Fourth Amendment protection. In a 2013 Fifth Circuit Court of Appeals case, the government sought access to two months of historical cell site location data, which provides the location of a cell phone based on its proximity to the nearest cell tower.[104] Noting this distinction between intermediary and recipient, the court found that cell site records are "clearly business records" for which the third-party doctrine should apply, as the cell provider is a party to the transaction; the location information is not transferred to anyone but the provider; and the location information is needed to route the call.[105] Like the Fifth Circuit, several lower courts have applied the third-party doctrine to hold that access to cell site location information is not a Fourth Amendment search.[106]

However, over the past several years, a growing number of judges have pushed back against government attempts to circumvent the Fourth Amendment warrant requirement when seeking information about an individual's cell phone location data. The District Court for the Eastern District of New York, for instance, found that while the third-party doctrine generally covers the type of location information produced by a cell phone call, the "cumulative" collection of 113 days of constant surveillance implicated sufficiently heightened privacy interests to warrant an exception to the third-party doctrine.[107] This argument is based on the "mosaic theory" of the Fourth Amendment, which holds that while short-term monitoring may not reveal anything overly private about an individual, the aggregation of this information can be much more revealing.[108] In an alternative approach, the Third Circuit Court of Appeals reasoned that a cell phone user does not "voluntarily" share his location with a cell phone provider "in any meaningful way," prohibiting application of the third-party doctrine, but held that it was left to the discretion of the magistrate judge whether a warrant would be required.[109]

A more recent legal problem facing the lower courts is determining whether the third-party doctrine should apply to "cell tower dumps." These are instances in which the government is looking for the cell phone records of *unknown* persons who may have made a cell phone call after a reported crime, say, a bank robbery. The government requests all the calls made from the nearest cell tower within a certain period of time.[110] The few courts that have addressed the issue have split on whether a warrant is required.[111] Thus far, the reasoning in these cases has not been fully developed.

Beyond the specific factors the courts have used to determine whether the third-party doctrine should apply (e.g., content versus non-content, intermediary versus recipient), there have been both doctrinal and practical arguments made for and against its very existence.

SUPPORT FOR THE THIRD-PARTY DOCTRINE

Perhaps the strongest argument in support of the third-party doctrine is its ability to be harmonized with the rest of Fourth Amendment case law. One only has to quickly scan the Supreme Court Reporter to realize that the third-party doctrine is consistent with numerous other cases which hold that acts or things revealed to the public are not entitled to Fourth Amendment protection.

Take, for instance, the garbage collection case, *California v. Greenwood*.[112] There, the police requested that a trash collector pick up a suspect's plastic trash bags left in front of his house so the officer could search it for contraband or other evidence of criminal activity. The Court concluded that the defendant was not entitled to a reasonable expectation of privacy in his trash as he discarded it where it could be accessed by the public.[113] Similarly, in *United States v. Knotts*, the Court held that a person does not have a legitimate privacy expectation in his public movements as he voluntarily conveys this information to anyone who wants to look.[114] This theory has also been applied to cases where police flew an airplane 1,000 feet and a helicopter 400 feet over private property in search of illegal activity.[115] The rationale in those cases was that any member of the public flying in federally regulated airspace could have looked down and seen what the officers saw, vitiating any privacy expectation in that space.[116] In *United States v. Jacobsen*, the Court held that it was not a search when police opened a mailed package after its contents had already been viewed by an employee of a private freight carrier.[117] There, the Court observed that once the defendant's privacy expectation had been frustrated by one person, it became public information subject to government investigation.[118]

As a more practical matter, assistance from third parties is utilized by law enforcement in almost every investigation. When investigating a murder, robbery, or any other crime committed in the real world, police officers will usually interview witnesses to obtain facts about the crime. To conduct these interviews, the officers generally need not obtain a warrant, and witnesses who refuse to cooperate can be compelled to testify with a grand jury subpoena.[119] It could be argued that this process of fact finding is very similar to requesting documentary evidence held by third parties and the same standard should be applied to each.

In this same vein, Professor Orin Kerr has defended the third-party doctrine on the ground that it maintains the appropriate balance of privacy and security in the face of technological change.[120] Without the ability to use third parties such as telephone or Internet companies, Kerr posits, the criminal would traditionally have to go out into the public to commit his crime where the Fourth Amendment offers more limited protection. He argues that a criminal can use the services of these third parties to commit crimes without having to expose these activities to areas open to public surveillance.[121] This, he posits, upsets the privacy-security balance that undergirds the Fourth Amendment because it would require police to have probable cause to obtain any evidence of the crime: "The effect would be a Catch-22: The police would need probable cause to observe evidence of the crime, but they would need to observe evidence of the crime first to get probable cause."[122] Kerr contends that the third-party doctrine responds to this imbalance by providing the same amount of protection regardless of whether the defendant commits the crime on his own or through the use of a third-party service.

From an institutional perspective, one might argue that the courts are not the proper branch of the federal government to resolve privacy disputes related to information handed over to third-parties. Once the Supreme Court outlaws, or significantly limits, a certain police practice, it "constitutionalizes" it, and only the Court or a constitutional amendment could overturn this decision. Instead, some argue that when creating rules that pertain to new technologies, Congress, and legislatures generally, might be best fitted to find the appropriate balance between privacy and security, while providing the necessary flexibility to change this rule as technology changes.[123]

Another argument in support of the third-party doctrine is that the companies which hold a person's records "own" them, as they are in possession of them and are generally the ones that create them.[124] Once possessed by the company, the argument runs, it can transfer these documents to others free from the permission of the subject of the documents. The Court relied on this theory in *Miller*, where it noted that the bank records were not the defendant's "private papers," and as such he could "assert neither ownership nor possession."[125] Instead, they were deemed "the business records of the banks."[126] This argument is buttressed by the theory that the First Amendment protects a person's right to communicate facts to others.[127]

CRITICISM OF THE THIRD-PARTY DOCTRINE

While the third-party doctrine appears to fit reasonably well with the rest of Fourth Amendment case law, and has other weighty arguments in its favor, it has also had its share of vocal critics both on and off the Court. There have been four major arguments against its application: (1) privacy is not an all-or-nothing proposition that is lost once information is disclosed to another person or company; (2) information sent to third-party companies is not actually "voluntary," as people need these services to participate in modern society; (3) the judiciary should not impose privacy regimes on the citizenry without engaging in a more comprehensive privacy analysis; and (4) failing to protect information shared with others has the potential to breed distrust among people or businesses communicating with each other.

The first major argument against the third-party doctrine challenges the notion that once privacy is lost to one person, it is lost to the world. At bottom, this is a challenge to the secrecy model of the Fourth Amendment. The secrecy theory of privacy has been criticized for not taking into consideration that people may not want to engage in "total disclosure" of information they share with others, but instead seek to selectively disclose that information.[128] Justice Marshall said as much in dissent in *Smith v. Maryland*,where he argued that "privacy is not a discrete commodity, possessed absolutely or not at all."[129] He continued: "Those who disclose certain facts to a bank or phone company for a limited business purpose need not assume that this information will be released to other persons for other purposes."[130] Several commentators have similarly argued that there is an important distinction between information that is broadcast to the world and that which is disclosed in a controlled environment.[131] The first category, they argue, includes instances where the government accesses information that is readily available in the public square, such as information posted on a publicly available website or a loud conversation overheard in an airport.[132] Because the person has decided to release this information to the public, he cannot later claim to have an expectation of privacy. The latter category, on the other hand, entails a more limited sharing that is "an integral part of a legitimate transaction" between the individual and the recipient of the information, and is entitled to Fourth Amendment protection.[133]

Along these same lines, some have pointed out the apparent inconsistency in Fourth Amendment protection accorded to various types of information people share with third parties. In *Katz v. United States* and *Berger v. New York*, the Court held that people have an expectation of privacy in the content of their conversations,[134] while similar protection was not extended to the telephone numbers dialed in *Smith*.[135] Dissenting in *Smith,* Justice Stewart, who authored the *Katz* majority opinion, pointed out this incongruity, noting that like telephone numbers, the voice of a conversation must be transmitted through the telephone company's equipment and may be overheard or recorded by that company.[136] He argued that "what the telephone company does or might do with those numbers is no more relevant to this inquiry than it would be in a case involving the conversation itself."[137] Instead, Justice Stewart would have granted both forms of information protection under *Katz*.[138] In a line that would foreshadow more recent arguments against the third-party doctrine, Justice Stewart contended that people are not concerned about revealing a list of their telephone calls because it could be incriminating, but rather because it would "reveal the most intimate details of a person's life."[139] The second major argument against the third-party doctrine challenges the idea that people "voluntarily" convey information to others when engaging in business transactions. In *Miller*, the Court asserted that the financial statements and deposit slips were "voluntarily conveyed" to the banks in the "ordinary course of business,"[140] and in *Smith* the defendant "voluntarily conveyed numerical information to the telephone company."[141] More recently, a federal court of appeals judge made a similar argument regarding cell phone users:

> Their use of their phones, moreover, is entirely voluntary. The Government does not require a member of the public to own or carry a phone. As the days of monopoly phone companies are past, the Government does not require him to obtain his cell phone service from a particular service provider that keeps historical cell site records for its subscribers, either. And it does not require him to make a call, let alone to make a call at a specific location.[142]

There has been significant disagreement, however, about how *voluntary* these transactions really are. Justice Brennan argued in dissent that "for all practical purposes, the disclosure by individuals or business firms of their financial affairs to a bank is not entirely volitional, since it is impossible to participate in the economic life of contemporary society without maintaining a bank account."[143] Similarly, Justice Marshall argued in *Smith* that "unless a person is prepared to forgo use" of the telephone, which for "many has become a personal or professional necessity, he cannot help but accept the risk of surveillance. It is idle to speak of 'assuming' risks in contexts where, as a practical matter, individuals have no realistic alternative."[144] One commentator has argued that unlike the undercover agent cases, where refusing to talk to a particular individual is a "realistic option," refusing to get medical treatment or an education would lead to an "unproductive" and "possibly much foreshortened existence."[145]

The third central argument against the third-party doctrine challenges the assertion that people "assume the risk" when handing information over to third parties. People do not assume legal risks as a matter of pure deduction, the argument goes, "but assume only those risks of unregulated government intrusion that the courts tell us we have to assume."[146] Dissenting in *White*, Justice Harlan expressed concern about the process by which courts determine how much privacy protection people should expect and will receive. He notes that people's expectations of privacy and the risks they assume are "reflections" of the laws handed down by courts or legislatures. Because it is the "task of the law to form and project, as well as mirror or reflect," Justice Harlan instructs, "we should not, as judges, merely recite the expectations and risks without examining the desirability of saddling them upon society."[147] Instead of allowing "the substitution of words for analysis," courts should assess "the nature of a particular practice and the likely extent of its impact on the individual's sense of security balanced against the utility of the conduct as a technique of law enforcement."[148] In other words, rather than simply applying the phrase "assumption of the risk" in each new legal context, Justice Harlan suggested that courts should look anew at each surveillance practice and determine its actual impact on the individual's privacy interests.[149] One commentator has suggested a similar approach in that the government should not have "practically unrestricted access" to people's records, or, on the flipside, that probable cause must be required for every request of documents. Instead, he argues that the level of protection should depend on the nature of the documents requested.[150] For example, certain types of records, including public records, may not be entitled to the same protection as others, such as medical or financial records.[151]

Lastly, many practical arguments have been formulated against application of third-party doctrine. Justice Harlan believed one of the main concerns with the third-party doctrine was its ability to breed distrust in people who are communicating with others. He noted that the practice of third-party bugging "undermine[s] the confidence and sense of security in dealing with one another that is characteristic of individual relationships between citizens in a free society."[152] In Justice Harlan's view, "words would be measured a good deal more carefully and communication inhibited if one suspected his conversations were being transmitted and transcribed."[153] One only has to look to the recent NSA controversy as a more modern example. Some argue that knowledge that information shared with tech companies like Google, Facebook, and Apple might end up in the hands of the government has the potential to engender distrust and cost American businesses significant revenues both at home and abroad.[154]

IMPLICATIONS OF *UNITED STATES V. JONES* ON THE THIRD-PARTY DOCTRINE

In addition to the doctrinal and practical arguments made against the third-party doctrine, several concurring opinions in the recent GPS tracking case *United States v. Jones* prompt additional questions about its continued application. Some argue that these opinions foreshadow a shift in the Court's thinking about the effect of technology on the government's ability to collect large data sets about American citizens.

In *Jones*, the police attached a GPS tracking device to the underbelly of Jones's car and tracked it 24 hours a day for 28 days without a warrant.[155]

Under controlling precedent, a person had no reasonable expectation of privacy when traveling on public streets because he has revealed his movements to the public at large.[156] While it appeared that *Jones* required a strict application of this previous case law, the Court ruled 9-0 against the government, and held that the investigative activity there constituted a Fourth Amendment search. The reason why, however, was far from unanimous.

The majority opinion, written by Justice Scalia, and joined by Chief Justice Roberts and Justices Kennedy, Thomas, and Sotomayor, held that the physical attachment of the tracking device on Jones's car, coupled with the intent to obtain information about his movements, amounted to a Fourth Amendment search.[157] When the police attached the device, they physically trespassed onto his vehicle, his "effect," a constitutionally protected area under the Fourth Amendment's protection of "persons, houses, papers, and effects."[158] As Justice Scalia's opinion relied upon a trespass theory of the Fourth Amendment, it will likely not have major repercussions for the third-party doctrine, unless one accepts that the government trespasses on an individual's "papers" or "effects" when it accesses records from third-party companies.[159]

However, two concurring opinions in *Jones* by Justices Sotomayor and Alito might signal the willingness of five Justices to reevaluate future applications of the third-party doctrine, at least with respect to pervasive government monitoring. Justice Sotomayor's solo concurrence provided the more far-reaching of the two opinions. She directly called into question "the premise that an individual has no reasonable expectation of privacy in information voluntarily disclosed to third parties."[160] She observed:

> This approach is ill suited to the digital age, in which people reveal a great deal of information about themselves to third parties in the course of carrying out mundane tasks. People disclose the phone numbers that they dial or text to their cellular providers; the URLs that they visit and the e-mail addresses with which they correspond to their Internet service providers; and the books, groceries, and medications they purchase to online retailers.... I for one doubt that people would accept without complaint the warrantless disclosure to the Government of a list of every Web site they had visited in the last week, or month, or year. But whatever the societal expectations, they can attain constitutionally protected status only if our Fourth Amendment jurisprudence ceases to treat secrecy as a prerequisite for privacy. I would not assume that all information voluntarily disclosed to some member of the public for a limited purpose is, for that reason alone, disentitled to Fourth Amendment protection.[161]

It seems that Justice Sotomayor, if not prepared to discard the third-party doctrine in whole, is willing to significantly limit its reach, especially when the government is accessing a wealth of data about an individual. Again, it should be noted that Justice Sotomayor was the only member to articulate this more expansive roll-back of the third-party doctrine.

More generally, both Justices Sotomayor and Alito's opinions could be interpreted to call into question the continued application of the third-party doctrine insofar as it permits pervasive government monitoring. In his concurrence, Justice Alito, joined by Justices Ginsburg, Breyer, and Kagan, found that while short-term monitoring may be permissible under past precedent, "the use of longer term GPS monitoring in investigations of most offenses impinges on expectations of privacy."[162] Justice Sotomayor, who joined the majority but also concurred separately, agreed with Justice Alito's approach and would have gone even further to find that short-term monitoring should be prohibited in some instances.[163]

These five Justices expressed two interrelated concerns. First, they were uneasy about the government's ability to gather, analyze, and use an extensive volume of information about each person's comings and goings. Justice Sotomayor observed that "GPS monitoring generates a precise, comprehensive records of a person's public movements that reflects a wealth of information about her familial, political, professional, religious, and sexual associations."[164] This idea, commonly referred to as the "mosaic theory," posits that the aggregation of information about a person can reveal a whole lot more about him than each part in isolation. The Justices were not the first to espouse this theory. Before the case reached the Supreme Court, the District of Columbia Court of Appeals below articulated a similar sentiment in finding that the government's month-long location tracking constituted a Fourth Amendment search:

> Prolonged surveillance reveals types of information not revealed by short-term surveillance, such as what a person does repeatedly, what he does not do, and what he does ensemble. These types of information can each reveal more about a person than does any individual trip viewed in isolation. Repeated visits to a church, a gym, a bar, or a bookie tell a story not told by any single visit, as does one's not visiting any of these places over the course of a month. The sequence of a person's movements can reveal still more; a single trip to a gynecologist's office tells little about a woman, but that trip followed a few weeks later by a visit to a baby supply store

> tells a different story. A person who knows all of another's travels can deduce whether he is a weekly church goer, a heavy drinker, a regular at the gym, an unfaithful husband, an outpatient receiving medical treatment, an associate of particular individuals or political groups—and not just one such fact about a person, but all such facts.[165]

In addition to this aggregation issue, the Justices expressed concern about the ability of technology to significantly reduce natural barriers such as limited resources and political accountability that in the past would have limited law enforcement overreach in the field of surveillance.[166] For Justice Alito, the fact that the government simply could not have tracked a person's every movement for a month-long period under traditional law enforcement methods led him to conclude that the tracking was overly intrusive.[167]

While Justice Sotomayor directly criticized the third-party doctrine, one could read Justice Alito's concurrence as limited solely to monitoring conducted directly by government agents, and not extending to instances where third parties collect data on individuals. That being said, the combination of the *Jones* concurrences has already had an effect in third-party cases in lower federal courts. For example, the District Court for the District of Columbia applied a variation of the mosaic theory to invalidate the NSA's collection of telephone call records.[168] Citing to the *Jones* concurrences, Judge Richard H. Leon acknowledged that the type of information collected under the NSA's metadata program was very similar to that upheld in *Smith*, "but the ubiquity of phones has dramatically altered the *quantity* of information that is now available and, *more importantly*, what that information can tell the Government about people's lives."[169] And, as described above, judges in certain cell phone location monitoring cases have applied *Jones* and the mosaic theory to deem months-long government tracking a Fourth Amendment search.[170] In the long run, it may take a more pertinent set of facts for the Justices to advance the arguments enunciated in *Jones*.

Congressional Response to the Third-Party Doctrine

Notwithstanding the concurring opinions in *Jones*, the bulk of Supreme Court and lower federal court precedent have left most non-content information unprotected by the Fourth Amendment. In some instances, Congress filled this void by creating varying levels of privacy protection for this type of non-content information. However, these protections are in the main not as robust as the warrant requirement, and in some instances, searches may be justified by little more than "official curiosity."[171]

Seven years after the Court handed down *Smith* and ruled that government access to telephone toll records was not covered by the Fourth Amendment, Congress enacted as part of the Electronic Communications Privacy Act of 1986 (ECPA) several provisions requiring the government to seek a court order before using a pen register or trap and trace device.[172] Again, these devices allow the government to gather dialed telephone numbers and email addressing information, among other non-content information.[173] Under 18 U.S.C. § 3123, a court "shall issue an ex parte order authorizing the installation and use of a pen register or trap and trace device ... if the court finds that the attorney for the Government has certified that the information likely to be obtained by such installation and use is relevant to an ongoing criminal investigation."[174]

A few things should be noted about this provision. First, the "shall" language removes discretion from the judge; if the judge finds the government has made the required certification, he must issue the order.[175] Second, while the court must ensure that the government has made the proper certification, ECPA does not require an "independent judicial inquiry into the veracity of the attested facts."[176] This means that the judge will not make an independent assessment whether the relevancy standard has been met, but only that the government has made the proper certification. One district court has noted that "the extremely limited judicial review required by [the pen register statute] is intended merely to safeguard against purely random use of this device."[177] One magistrate judge went so far as to describe his role under the pen register statute as a "rubber stamp" limited to "proofreading errors," and that "without independent judicial review, the authorization of pen registers is subject to misuse and abuse."[178] Third, the relevancy standard, which again the government, and not the court, determines if it has been met, is a "far from burdensome" legal standard.[179] The Supreme Court has held, at least in the subpoena context, that information sought is not relevant only if "there is no reasonable possibility that the category of materials the Government seeks will produce information relevant to the general subject" of the investigation.[180] In light of this relatively lax standard, several prominent commentators on privacy and technology have suggested that Congress should increase the evidentiary threshold under Section 3123 from mere relevance to at least a reasonable suspicion standard similar to that used for accessing certain stored communications.[181]

Also included in ECPA is the Stored Communications Act (SCA), in which Congress provided varying degrees of protection to information historically subject to the third-party doctrine and, thus, outside the reach of the Fourth Amendment. Under 18 U.S.C. § 2703(c), service providers must hand over "records or other information pertaining to a subscriber" so long as the government can establish "specific and articulable facts" that the records are "relevant and material" to an ongoing criminal investigation.[182] This is akin to the *Terry* reasonable suspicion standard—it is lower than probable cause but does require the government to articulate its basis to believe that the information is connected to criminal activity.[183] This standard has been applied to data such as the to/from address line in an email or the IP addresses of websites a person has visited. Some courts have construed Section 2703(d) in conjunction with the pen register statute to allow the government access to cell site location information.[184] Section 2703(c)(2) requires the providers to hand over other customer information such as their name, address, telephone calling records, length of service, telephone number, and means and source of payments, including credit card or bank account numbers with either an administrative, grand jury, or trial subpoena.[185]

Additionally, Congress has passed more targeted privacy protection laws. For instance, the privacy of cable subscribers is safeguarded under the Cable Communications Privacy Act of 1984,[186] and the privacy of video store customers under the Video Privacy Protection Act.[187]

More recently, various Members of Congress have sought to temper the reach of the third-party doctrine with respect to transactional data. Several days after the Edward Snowden leaks became public, Senator Paul filed the "Fourth Amendment Restoration Act of 2013" (S. 1121) in an effort to "stop the National Security Agency from spying on citizens of the United States[.]"[188] This bill would require that "[t]he Fourth Amendment to the Constitution shall not be construed to allow any agency of the United States Government to search the phone records of Americans without a warrant based upon probable cause."[189] While dictating to the judiciary what the Fourth Amendment should and should not protect may be beyond Congress's constitutional power,[190] Congress clearly can play a role in setting substantive and procedural limitations on government surveillance authorities. For instance, Senator Paul has introduced a similar bill, the "Fourth Amendment Preservation and Protection Act of 2013" (S. 1037), which would prohibit federal, state, and local government officials from accessing information relating to an individual held by a third party in a "system of records."[191] Other congressional measures would alter the third-party doctrine in a more targeted way. Several location monitoring bills would, for instance, prohibit companies from sharing their customers' location information unless the government obtained a warrant or one of several limited exceptions applied.[192]

CONCLUSION

So what does the future have in store for the third-party doctrine and the government's collection of non-content, transactional data? At this point, there appears to be only one solid vote on the Court in Justice Sotomayor for eliminating or significantly reducing the scope of this doctrine. Although there are hints in Justice Alito's *Jones* opinion that he and the three members of his concurrence are ready to reconsider this rule when it comes to pervasive government surveillance, his rationale was left somewhat underdeveloped. It will take future opinions to get a better sense of whether or how far these Justices are willing to go to limit government access to non-content information held in the hands of third parties. In the meantime, the lower federal courts might continue to limit or distinguish the third-party doctrine in specific and narrow instances. For instance, in the NSA telephone metadata case, Judge Leon limited *Smith* to its facts and held that it did not apply to this more comprehensive data collection program.[193] Likewise, if and when the Supreme Court is asked to reconsider the scope of the third-party doctrine, it is more likely to carve out specific exceptions than to overturn it in its entirety. This approach would permit the courts to engage in a more nuanced, normative approach to analyzing the privacy interests implicated by accessing records derived from transactions between people and other various entities.

Another possibility is for Congress to act. Justice Alito observed in *Jones* that "[i]in circumstances involving dramatic technological change, the best solution to privacy concerns may be legislative" as "a legislative body is well situated to gauge changing public attitudes, to draw detailed lines, and to balance privacy and public safety in a comprehensive way."[194] This argument that Congress is best suited to address the nuanced policy questions that privacy and security entails has been expressed by commentators as well.[195] Like the courts, it appears unlikely that Congress would be willing to completely eliminate the third-party doctrine. On the other hand, Congress may be more inclined to engage in a subject-by-subject approach, in which Congress limits the third-party doctrine in certain areas. Congress provided statutory protection for telephone toll records in the pen register/trap and trace statute; for Internet metadata in the Stored Communications Act; and for video customer records in the Video Privacy Protection Act. It could enact similar protection for other subject areas where non-content information is shared with companies as a necessary part of doing business.

End Notes

[1] Katz v. United States, 389 U.S. 347, 351 (1967).

[2] Smith v. Maryland, 442 U.S. 735, 743-44 (1979).

[3] *See, e.g.*, Orin Kerr and Greg Nojeim, *The Data Question: Should the Third-Party Records Doctrine Be Revisited?*, ABA JOURNAL (Aug. 1, 2012), *available at* http://www.abajournal.com/magazine/article/ the_data_question_should_the_third-party_records_doctrine_be_revisited/; Orin Kerr, *The Case for the Third Party Doctrine*, 107 MICH. L. REV. 561, 575 (2009); Richard A. Epstein, *Privacy and the Third Hand: Lessons from the Common Law of Reasonable Expectations*, 24 BERKELEY TECH. L. J. 1199 (2009); Erin Murphy, *The Case Against the Case for Third-Party Doctrine: A Response to Epstein and Kerr*, 24 BERKELEY TECH. L. J. 1239 (2009); Stewart Baker, Smith v. Maryland *as a Good First-Order Estimate of Reasonable Privacy Expectations*, VOLOKH CONSPIRACY (May 4, 2014), *available at* http://www.washingtonpost.com /news/volokh-conspiracy/

[4] *See infra* notes 49-66, and accompanying cases.

[5] United States v. Miller, 425 U.S. 435 (1976); *Smith*, 442 U.S. 735.

[6] *Katz*, 389 U.S. at 352 (voice); United States v. Warshak, 631 F.3d 266, 288 (6th Cir. 2010) (email).

[7] *See, e.g.*, United States v. Miller, 425 U.S. 435, 447 (Brennan, J., dissenting); Stephen E. Henderson, *The Timely Demise of the Fourth Amendment Third Party Doctrine*, 96 IOWA L. REV. BULL. 396 (2011); CHRISTOPHER SLOBOGIN, PRIVACY AT RISK: THE NEW GOVERNMENT SURVEILLANCE AND THE FOURTH AMENDMENT 140 (2007).

[8] California v. Greenwood, 486 U.S. 35, 43-44 (1988).

[9] United States v. Knotts, 460 U.S. 276, 285 (1983).

[10] Florida v. Riley, 488 U.S. 445, 451-52 (1989).

[11] *See* DANIEL J. SOLOVE, THE DIGITAL PERSON: TECHNOLOGY AND PRIVACY IN THE INFORMATION AGE 202 (2004) ("The government's harvesting of information from the extensive dossiers being assembled with modern computer technology poses one of the most significant threats to privacy of our time.").

[12] Omer Tene and Jules Polonetsky, *Big Data for All: Privacy and User Controls in the Age of Analytics*, 11 NW. J. TECH. & INTELL. PROP. 239, *1(2013) ("Big data is upon us." https://a.next.westlaw.com/Document/I535f4a8bb78611e28578f7ccc38dcbee/View/Full Text.html?navigationPath= Search%2Fv3%2Fsearch%2Fresults%2Fnavigation%2Fi0ad60 40300000146014bbf3f6cbb1298%3FNav%3DANALY TICAL%26fragmentIdentifier%3DI 535f4a8bb78611e28578f7ccc38dcbee%26startIndex%3D1%26contextData%3D%2528 sc.Search%2529%26transitionType%3DSearchItem&listSource=Search&listPageSource= 4f65f444bd87ab8451abbca5a750d542&list=ANALYTICAL&rank=10&grading =na&

sessionScopeId= bbd4e55d34300e25e857bc0ccd7bbb05&originationContext=Search%20Result&transitionType=SearchItem&contextData=%28sc.Search%29-co_footnote_F3388167494 Over the past few years, the volume of data collected and stored by business and government organizations has exploded. The trend is driven by reduced costs of storing information and moving it around in conjunction with increased capacity to instantly analyze heaps of unstructured data using modern experimental methods, observational and longitudinal studies, and large scale simulations. Data are generated from online transactions, email, video, images, clickstream, logs, search queries, health records, and social networking interactions; gleaned from increasingly pervasive sensors deployed in infrastructure such as communications networks, electric grids, global positioning satellites, roads and bridges, as well as in homes, clothing, and mobile phones.").

[13] United States v. Jones, 132 S. Ct. 945 (2012).

[14] *Id.* at 954 (Sotomayor, J., concurring); *Id.* at 957 (Alito, J., concurring).

[15] *See, e.g.,* Priscilla J. Smith, *Much Ado About Mosaics: How Original Principles Apply to Evolving Technology in* United States v. Jones, 14 N.C. J.L. & TECH 557, 571 (2013); David Gray & Danielle Keats Citron, *A Shattered Looking Glass: The Pitfalls and Potential of the Mosaic Theory of Fourth Amendment Privacy*, 14 N.C. J. L. & Tech. 381 (2013).

[16] ACLU v. Clapper, 959 F. Supp. 2d 724 (S.D.N.Y. 2013); Smith v. Obama, No. 2:13-CV-257 (D. Idaho June 3, 2014); *In re* Application of the Fed. Bureau of Investigation for an Order Requiring the Production of Tangible Things from [Redacted], No. BR 13-109 (FISA Ct. 2013), *available at* http://www.uscourts.gov/uscourts/courts/fisc/br13-09- primary-order.pdf.

[17] Klayman v. Obama, 957 F. Supp. 2d 1, 36 (D.D.C. 2013).

[18] Thomas K. Clancy, *What is a "Search" Within the Meaning of the Fourth Amendment*, 70 ALB. L. REV. 1, 4 (2006) ("The abhorred English and colonial search and seizure practices involved physical invasions of people's property. That was not surprising given that physical invasions were the only way authorities could intrude at the time and given the lack of technology and other sophisticated surveillance techniques."); *see generally* WILLIAM J. CUDDIHY, THE FOURTH AMENDMENT: ORIGINS AND MEANING 602-1791 (2009).

[19] *See* Thomas K. Clancy, *The Role of Individualized Suspicion in Assessing the Reasonableness of Searches and Seizures*, 25 U. MEM. L. REV. 483, 501-512 (1995) (discussing early English and American search and seizure case law).

[20] Entick v. Carrington, 95 Eng. Rep. 807, 807 (C.P. 1765).

[21] *Id.*

[22] *Id.* at 817.

[23] Cuddihy, *supra* note 18, at 380.

[24] *Id.*

[25] Brief of James Otis, MASSACHUSETTS SPY, Apr. 29, 1773, at 3.

[26] 1 JOHN ADAMS & CHARLES FRANCIS ADAMS, THE WORKS OF JOHN ADAMS: SECOND PRESIDENT OF THE UNITED STATES 57 (1856).

[27] U.S. CONST. amend. IV.

[28] *See* Scott E. Sundby, *A Return to Fourth Amendment Basics: Undoing the Mischief of* Camara *and* Terry, 72 MINN. L. REV. 383, 383-84 (1988).

[29] United States v. Boyd, 116 U.S. 616 (1886).

[30] *Id.*

[31] *Id.*

[32] Olmstead v. United States, 277 U.S. 438 (1928).

[33] *Id.* at 466.
[34] *Id.* at 476 (Brandeis, J, dissenting).
[35] *Id.* at 478 (Brandeis, J, dissenting).
[36] Goldman v. United States, 316 U.S. 129, 135 (1942).
[37] Silverman v. United States, 365 U.S. 505, 511-12 (1961).
[38] Katz v. United States, 389 U.S. 347 (1967).
[39] *Id.* at 349.
[40] *Id.* at 351.
[41] *Id.* at 350.
[42] *Id.* at 351, 353.
[43] *Id.* at 360 (Harlan, J., concurring); *see* Kyllo v. United States, 533 U.S. 27, 32-33 (2001) ("In assessing when a search is not a search, we have applied somewhat in reverse the principle first enunciated in *Katz v. United States*. ... As Justice Harlan's oft-quoted concurrence described it, a Fourth Amendment search occurs when the government violates a subjective expectation of privacy that society recognizes as reasonable.").
[44] *Id.* at 361 (Harlan, J. concurring).
[45] *Katz*, 389 U.S. at 351-52.
[46] Solove, *supra* note 11, at 8.
[47] *Ex parte* Jackson, 96 U.S. 727, 736 (1877).
[48] *See* United States v. Lee, 274 U.S. 559 (1927); *see also* United States v. Martin, 806 F.2d 204, 207 (8th Cir. 1986) ("[I]t was inappropriate to subject the agent's conduct of looking through the window of the truck to Fourth Amendment scrutiny in the first place. The agent's mere observation of gun parts left in plain view on the front seat of the truck did not implicate any Fourth Amendment rights.").
[49] On Lee v. United States, 343 U.S. 747, 748 (1952).
[50] *Id.* at 751-52.
[51] Lopez v. United States, 373 U.S. 427, 430 (1963).
[52] *Id.* at 437.
[53] *Id.* at 439.
[54] Lewis v. United States, 385 U.S. 206 (1966).
[55] *Id* at 210, 212.
[56] Hoffa v. United States, 385 U.S. 293, 296 (1966).
[57] *Id.* at 302.
[58] *See Lopez*, 373 U.S. at 439 ("And the device was not planted by means of an unlawful physical invasion of petitioner's premises under circumstances that would violate the Fourth Amendment.").
[59] *See* On Lee, 343 U.S. at 751-52.
[60] *Hoffa*, 385 U.S. at 302 ("[The government agent] was in the suite by invitation, and every conversation which he heard was either directed to him or knowingly carried on in his presence."); *Lopez*, 373 U.S. at 438 ("The only evidence obtained consisted of statements made by the [defendant] to the [government agent], statements which [the defendant] knew full well could be used against him by [the government agent] if he wished.").
[61] *Hoffa*, 385 U.S. at 302.
[62] *See* 1 WAYNE R. LAFAVE, SEARCH AND SEIZURE § 2.2(f) (2004).
[63] United States v. White, 401 U.S. 745, 746-47 (1971).
[64] United States v. White, 405 F.2d 838 (7th Cir. 1969).
[65] *White*, 401 U.S. at 750 (quoting *On Lee*, 343 U.S. at 753-54) ("It would be a dubious service to the genuine liberties protected by the Fourth Amendment to make them bedfellows with

spurious liberties improvised by farfetched analogies which would liken eavesdropping on a conversation, with the connivance of one of the parties, to an unreasonable search or seizure.")).

[66] *Id.* at 752 ("Inescapably, one contemplating illegal activities must realize that his companions may be reporting to the police."). Assumption of the risk is more commonly found in the context of tort law, where a person assumes certain risks that accompany the activities he is engaged in. *See* Murphy v. Steeplechase Amusements Co., 250 N.Y. 479 (1929) (Cardozo, J.) ("Volenti non fit injuria. One who takes part in such a sport accepts the dangers that inhere in it so far as they are obvious and necessary, just as a fencer accepts the risk of a thrust by his antagonist or a spectator at a ball game the chance of contact with the ball.").

[67] While primarily concerned with the Fifth Amendment right to self-incrimination, *Couch v. United States*, 409 U.S. 322, 335(1973), observed that "there can be little expectation of privacy where [tax] records are handed to an accountant, knowing that mandatory disclosure of much of the information therein is required in an income tax return.").

[68] United States v. Miller, 425 U.S. 435 (1976); Smith v. Maryland, 442 U.S. 735 (1979).

[69] *Miller*, 425 U.S. at 437.

[70] *Id.* at 438.

[71] *Id.*

[72] *Miller*, 425 U.S. at 441 (quoting California Bankers Assn. v. Shultz, 416 U.S. 21, 54 (1974)).

[73] *See California Bankers Ass'n*, 416 U.S. at 54 n.24.

[74] *Miller*, 425 U.S. at 442 (quoting Katz v. United States, 389 U.S. 347, 351 (1967)).

[75] *Id.*

[76] *Id.* at 443.

[77] *Id.* at 443.

[78] Smith v. Maryland, 442 U.S. 735 (1979).

[79] *Id.* at 737.

[80] Smith v. Maryland, 283 Md. 156, 173 (1978).

[81] *Smith*, 442 U.S. at 740.

[82] *Id.* at 742.

[83] *Id.* at 742-43

[84] *Id.* at 743 (quoting *Katz*, 389 U.S. at 361).

[85] *Id.* at 743-44.

[86] *Id.* at 744.

[87] *Id.*

[88] *Ex parte* Jackson, 96 U.S. 727, 733 (1877); *see also* United States v. Jacobsen, 466 U.S. 109, 114 (1984) ("Letters and other sealed packages are in the general class of effects in which the public at large has a legitimate expectation of privacy; warrantless searches of such effects are presumptively unreasonable").

[89] Katz v. United States, 389 U.S. 347, 352 (1967).

[90] *Smith*, 442 U.S. at 741 (quoting United States v. New York Tel. Co. 434 U.S. 159, 167 (1977)).

[91] United States v. Warshak, 631 F.3d 266, 288 (6th Cir. 2010); *see also* City of Ontario v. Quon, 560 U.S. 746, 757 (2010) (assuming that petitioner had reasonable expectation of privacy in content of emails).

[92] *Id.* at 286.

[93] United States v. Forrester, 512 F.3d 500, 510 (9th Cir. 2007).

[94] *Id.* at 510.

[95] *Id.*

[96] See *In Re* of Applications of the United States of America for Orders (1) Authorizing the Use of Pen Registers and Trap and Trace Devices and (2) Authorizing Release of Subscriber Information, 515 F. Supp. 2d 325, 339 (E.D.N.Y. 2007); *see also In re* Application of the United States of America for an Order Authorizing (1) Installation and Use of a Pen Register and Trap and Trace Device or Process, (2) Access to Customer Records, and (3) Cell Phone Tracking, 441 F. Supp. 2d 816, (S.D. Tex. 2006) (deciding case on statutory grounds but noting constitutional concern with access to post-cut-through dialed digits without a warrant based upon probable cause).

[97] *In re Application for Subscriber Information*, 515 F. Supp. 2d at 336.

[98] *Forrester*, 512 F.3d at 510.

[99] *Warshak*, 631 F.3d at 286.

[100] *Id.*

[101] *Id.*

[102] *Id.* at 288.

[103] *Id.* (emphasis in original).

[104] *In re* Application of the United States of America for Historical Cell Site Data, 724 F.3d 600, 602 (5th Cir. 2013).

[105] *Id.* at 612.

[106] *See, e.g., In re* Application of the United States of America for an Order for Disclosure of Telecommunications Records and Authorizing the Use of a Pen Register and Trap and Trace, 405 F. Supp. 2d 435, 449-50 (S.D.N.Y. 2005); United States v. Graham, 846 F. Supp. 2d 384, 403 (D. Mar. 2012); United States v. Benford, No. 2:09-CR-86, 2010 WL 1266507 (N.D. Ind. 2010).

[107] *In re* Application of the United States of America for an Order Authorizing the Release of Historical Cell-Site Information, 809 F. Supp. 2d 113, 126 (E.D.N.Y. 2011).

[108] See *infra* "Implications of *United States v. Jones* on the Third-Party Doctrine," pp. 21-23.

[109] *See In re* Application of the United States of America for an Order Directing a Provider of Electronic Communication Service to Disclose Records to the Government, 620 F.3d 304, 317-18 (3d 2010).

[110] *See* Brian L. Owsley, *The Fourth Amendment Implications of the Government's Use of Cell Tower Dumps in Its Electronic Surveillance*, 16 U. PA. J. CONST. L. 1, 1-2 (2013).

[111] *Compare In re* Application of the United States of America for an Order Pursuant to 18 U.S.C. § 2703(d), 964 F. Supp. 2d 674, 678 (denying access to cell tower dump records) *with* United States v. Capito, No. 3:10-CR-8050 (D. Ariz Sept 14, 2011) (upholding access to cell tower dump records).

[112] California v. Greenwood, 486 U.S. 35, 37 (1988).

[113] *Id.* at 42.

[114] United States v. Knotts, 460 U.S. 276, 281-82 (1983).

[115] California v. Ciraolo, 476 U.S. 207, 213-14 (1986) (airplane); Florida v. Riley, 488 U.S. 445, 455 (1989) (helicopter).

[116] *Ciraolo*, 476 U.S. at 213-214; *Riley*, 488 U.S. at 451.

[117] United States v. Jacobsen, 466 U.S. 109, 117-18 (1984).

[118] *Id.* at 117. Like the Fourth Amendment, under the privacy tort of intrusion upon seclusion, which subjects one to liability for intruding upon the solitude or seclusion of another, there is no liability for observing or taking a person's photograph in public for his appearance is "open to the public eye." RESTATEMENT (SECOND) OF TORTS § 652B cmt. b (2013).

[119] United States v. Dionisio, 410 U.S. 1, 9-10 (1973) (observing the "historically grounded obligation of every person to appear and give his evidence before the grand jury. 'The

personal sacrifice involved is a part of the necessary contribution of the individual to the welfare of the public.' And while the duty may be 'onerous' at times, it is 'necessary to the administration of justice.'").

[120] *See* Orin Kerr, *The Case for the Third Party Doctrine*, 107 MICH. L. REV. 561, 575 (2009).

[121] *Id.*

[122] *Id.* at 576.

[123] *See* Orin Kerr, *The Fourth Amendment and New Technologies: Constitutional Myths and the Case for Caution*, 102 MICH. L. REV. 801, 859 (2004).

[124] Slobogin, *supra* note 7, at 157 (describing arguments for and against the possessory interest argument).

[125] United States v. Miller, 425 U.S. 435, 440-41 (1976)

[126] *Id.*

[127] *See* Eugene Volokh, *Freedom of Speech and Information Privacy: The Troubling Implications of a Right to Stop People from Speaking About You*, 52 STAN. L. REV. 1049, 1053 (2000).

[128] See *Kenneth L. Karst, "The Files": Legal Controls Over the Accuracy and Accessibility of Stored Personal Data*, 31 LAW & CONTEMP. PROBS. 342, 344 (1966).

[129] *Smith*, 442 U.S. at 749 (Marshall, J., dissenting).

[130] *Id.*

[131] Susan W. Brenner & Leo L. Clarke, *Fourth Amendment for Shared Privacy Rights in Stored Transactional Data*, 14 J.L. & POL'Y 211, 258 (2006).

[132] *Id.*

[133] *Id.* This idea that a person loses all Fourth Amendment protection in information he shares with another would seem to be undermined by various cases in which shared information or spaces did not lose constitutional protection. For instance, in *Minnesota v. Olson*, the Court held that an overnight guest could have a reasonable expectation of privacy in the home of his host, "a place where he and his possessions will not be disturbed by anyone but his host and those his host allows inside."[133] On the other hand, these cases took place in the context of the home, an area accorded the highest Fourth Amendment protection, and their holdings might not easily extend to other contexts.

[134] Katz v. United States, 389 U.S. 347, 353 (1967); Berger v. New York, 388 U.S. 41, 51 (1967).

[135] *Smith*, 442 U.S. at 745.

[136] *Id,* at 746 (Stewart, J., dissenting).

[137] *Id.* at 747 (1979) (Stewart, J., dissenting).

[138] *Id.*

[139] *Id.* at 748 (Stewart, J., dissenting).

[140] United States v. Miller, 425 U.S. 435, 442 (1976).

[141] *Smith*, 442 U.S. 442 U.S. 744.

[142] *In re* Application of the United States of America for Historical Cell Site Data, 724 F.3d 600, 613 (5th Cir. 2013) (internal citation omitted),

[143] United States v. Miller, 425 U.S. 435, 451 (1973) (Brennan, J., dissenting) (quoting Burrows v. Superior Court, 13 Cal. 3d 238, 247 (1974)).

[144] *Smith*, 442 U.S. at 750 (Marshall, J., dissenting).

[145] Slobogin, *supra* note 7, at 156.

[146] *Id.* at 157; *see also* Stephen E. Henderson, *The Timely Demise of the Fourth Amendment Third Party Doctrine*, 96 IOWA L. REV. BULL. 39, 47 ("It is the law that defines what risks we do and do not assume.") .

[147] *White*, 401 U.S. at 786 (Harlan, J., concurring). A similar, and more general, criticism has been posed against the *Katz* 's reasonable expectation of privacy test. Some have argued

that it in determining which expectations of privacy are reasonable, judges are merely imposing their own views of privacy on society. *See* United States v. Jones, 132 S. Ct. 945, 962 (2012) (Alito, J., concurring) ("The *Katz* expectation-of-privacy test ... is not without its own difficulties. It involves a degree of circularity, and judges are apt to confuse their own expectations of privacy with those of the hypothetical reasonable person to which the *Katz* test looks."); Minnesota v. Carter, 525 U.S. 83, 97 (1998) (Scalia, J., concurring) ("In my view, the only thing the past three decades have established about the *Katz* test ... is that, unsurprisingly, those 'actual (subjective) expectation[s] of privacy' 'that society is prepared to recognize as 'reasonable,'' bear an uncanny resemblance to those expectations of privacy that this Court considers reasonable.").

[148] *United States v. White*, 401 U.S. 745, 786 (1971) (Harlan, J., concurring).

[149] *See* Catherine Hancock, *Warrants for Wearing a Wire: Fourth Amendment Privacy and Justice Harlan's Dissent in United States v. White*, 79 MISS. L. J. 35 (2009). Similar to Justice Harlan's comments, the majority in *Smith v. Maryland* observed that if people's subjective expectations of privacy becomes conditioned by government practices that were "alien to well-recognized Fourth Amendment freedoms," that a "normative inquiry would be proper" in determining what constituted a "legitimate expectation of privacy." *Smith*, 442 U.S. at 740-41 n.5.

[150] Slobogin, *supra* note 7, at 157.

[151] Slobogin, *supra* note 7, at 157.

[152] *White*, 401 U.S. at 787 (Harlan, J., dissenting).

[153] *Id.*

[154] *See* John Naughton, *Edward Snowden's Not the Story, the Internet Is*, THE GUARDIAN (July 23, 2013), *available at* http://www.theguardian.com/technology Allan Holmes, *NSA Spying Disclosures Could Cost Companies Billions* (Sept. 10, 2013), *available at* http://www.salon.com/2013/09/10/nsa_spying_disclosures_could_cost_companies_billions_in_sales_newscred/.

[155] United States v. Jones, 132 S. Ct. 945, 948 (2012). The D.C. Metropolitan police had obtained a warrant, but it had expired the day before the device was installed and was installed in the wrong jurisdiction. *Id.* at n.1.

[156] United States v. Knotts, 460 U.S. 276, 281 (1983).

[157] *Jones*, 132 S. Ct. at 949.

[158] *Id.* at 949; U.S. CONST. amend. IV.

[159] *See* Smith, *supra* note 15, at 571 ("One possibility is that Scalia's physical trespass analysis applies to digital trespass. After all, if an agent were to digitally connect with your computer, GPS device, or mobile phone for investigatory purposes, she is appropriating your property for purposes of gathering evidence, just like the agents who placed the tracker on your car."); Jack Wade Nowlin, *The Warren Court's House Built on Sand: From Security in Persons, Houses, Papers, and Effects to Mere Reasonableness in Fourth Amendment Doctrine*, 81 MISS. L. J. 1017, 1046-47 (2012) ("On the 'protected interest' view, one would retain one's right to security in the papers against governmental intrusion. The essence of the traditional security in protected interests, grounded in the law of property, is the right to exclude—which, of course, includes the right to selectively include some individuals while excluding others. On this view, one has a right to allow some actors access to one's home or papers while still excluding others— such as the police. It would thus invade the core of the protected interest for the government to obtain papers through a third party and search through them—without the owner's permission.").

[160] *Jones*, 132 S. Ct. at 957 (Sotomayor, J., concurring).

[161] *Id.*

[162] *Jones*, 132 S. Ct. at 964 (Alito, J., concurring).

[163] *Id.* at 957 (Sotomayor, J., concurring).

[164] Jones, 132 S. Ct. at 955.

[165] United States v. Maynard, 615 F.3d 544, 562 (D.C. Cir. 2010).

[166] *See* Jones 132 S. Ct. at 956 (Sotomayor, J., concurring) ("And because GPS monitoring is cheap in comparison to conventional surveillance techniques and, by design, proceeds surreptitiously, it evades the ordinary checks that constrain abusive law enforcement practices: 'limited police resources and community hostility.'") (quoting Illinois v. Lidster, 540 U.S. 419, 426 (2004)).

[167] *Jones*, 132 S. Ct. at 964 (Alito, J., concurring).

[168] Klayman v. Obama, 957 F. Supp. 2d 1, 36 (D.D.C. 2013).

[169] *Id.* at 35-36.

[170] *In re* Application of the United States of America for an Order Authorizing the Release of Historical Cell-Site Information, 809 F. Supp. 2d 113, 126 (E.D.N.Y. 2011).

[171] *See* United States v. Morton Salt Co., 338 U.S. 632, 652 (1950) (describing relevancy standard for subpoenas).

[172] Electronic Communications Privacy Act of 1986, P.L. 99-508, § 301, 100 Stat 1848.

[173] As enacted in 1986, the pen register statute, by its terms, only authorized the interception of *telephone* metadata. 100 Stat. 1871 ("[T]he term 'pen register' means a device which records or decodes electronic or other impulses which identify the numbers dialed or otherwise transmitted on the *telephone line* to which such device is attached.") (emphasis added). Congress extended the pen register/trap and trace authority to also cover Internet addressing information as part of the United and Strengthening America by Providing Appropriate Tools Required to Intercept and Obstruct Terrorism (USA PATRIOT Act) of 2001, P.L. 107-56, §216, 115 Stat. 272, 288, *codified at* 18 U.S.C. § 3127.

[174] 18 U.S.C. § 3123.

[175] *See* United States v. Fregoso, 60 F.3d 1314, 1320 (8th Cir. 1995) ("The judicial role in approving use of trap and trace devices is ministerial in nature because, upon a proper application being made under 18 U.S.C. § 3122, 'the court shall enter an ex parte order authorizing the installation' of such a device. 18 U.S.C. § 3123(a)") (emphasis in original)).

[176] *In re* Application of the United States of America for an Order Authorizing the Installation and Use of a Pen Register and Trap and Trace Device, 846 F. Supp. 1555, 1559 (M.D. Fla. 1994); *see also* S. Rpt. 99-541, at 47 (1986) ("[Section 3123] does not envision an independent judicial review of whether the application meets the relevance standard, rather the court needs only to review the completeness of the certification submitted.").

[177] United States v. Hallmark, 911 F.2d 399, 402 (10th 1990).

[178] *In re* Application of the United States of America for an Order Authorizing the Installation and Use of a Pen Register and Trap and Trace Device, 846 F. Supp. 1555, 1564-65, 1563 n.4 (M.D. Fla. 1994).

[179] *In Re* of Applications of the United States of America for Orders (1) Authorizing the Use of Pen Registers and Trap and Trace Devices and (2) Authorizing Release of Subscriber Information, 515 F. Supp. 2d 325, 329 (E.D.N.Y. 2007).

[180] United States v. R. Enterprises, Inc., 498 U.S. 292, 301 (1991).

[181] *See Anti-Terrorism Investigations and the Fourth Amendment After September 11, 2001: Hearing Before the Subcomm. on the Constitution of the H. Comm. of the Judiciary*, 108th Cong. 21, 26 (2003) (statements of James Dempsey, Center for Democracy and Technology, and Orin S. Kerr, Law Professor).

[182] 18 U.S.C. § 2703(d).

[183] *In re* Application of the United States of America for an Order Pursuant to 18 U.S.C. § 2703(d), 707 F.3d 283, 287 (4th Cir. 2013).

[184] *In re* Application of the United States of America for an Order for Disclosure of Telecommunications Records and Authorizing the Use of a Pen Register and Trap and Trace, 405 F. Supp. 2d 435, 449-50 (S.D.N.Y. 2005).

[185] 18 U.S.C. § 2703(c)(2).

[186] 47 U.S.C. § 551; *see* Kerr, *supra* note 123, at 855 ("A broader look at the legal standards that govern criminal investigations involving new technologies suggests that Congress has often taken the lead, and that judicial decisions interpreting the Fourth Amendment generally have played a secondary role").

[187] 18 U.S.C. § 2710.

[188] Fourth Amendment Restoration Act of 2013, S. 1121 (1st Sess. 2013).

[189] *Id.*

[190] *See* Dickerson v. United States, 530 U.S. 428, 437 (2000) ("Congress may not legislatively supersede our decisions interpreting and applying the Constitution.").

[191] Fourth Amendment Preservation and Protection Act of 2013, S. 1037, 113th Cong. (1st Sess. 2013).

[192] *See, e.g.*, Geolocation Privacy and Surveillance Act, S. 639, H.R. 1312, 113th Cong (1st Sess. 2013).

[193] *Klayman*, 957 F. Supp. 2d at 37 ("[T]he *Smith* pen register and the ongoing NSA Bulk Telephony Metadata Program have so many significant distinctions between them that I cannot possibly navigate these uncharted Fourth Amendment waters using as my North Star a case that predates the rise of cell phones.").

[194] *Jones*, 132 S. Ct. at 964.

[195] Kerr, *supra* note 123, at 857.

In: The Fourth Amendment
Editor: Lucille E. Huff
ISBN: 978-1-63321-634-1

Chapter 2

CLOUD COMPUTING: CONSTITUTIONAL AND STATUTORY PRIVACY PROTECTIONS*

Richard M. Thompson II

SUMMARY

Cloud computing is fast becoming an integral part of how we communicate with one another, buy music, share photos, conduct business, pay our bills, shop, and bank. Many of the activities that once occurred solely in the physical world, including communications with one another, are increasingly moving to the digital world. What was once a letter to a friend is now a Facebook message; a call to a loved one is now a Skype chat; a private meeting with a business partner is now a video conference call. In short, the cloud is revolutionizing not only how we compute, but also how we live. Where individuals once locked personal or business papers solely in a desk drawer or filing cabinet, they now also store them on someone else's computer.

In short, cloud computing is a web-based service that allows users to access anything from e-mail to social media on a third-party computer. For instance, Gmail and Yahoo are cloud-based email services that allow users to access and store emails that are saved on each respective service's computer, rather than on the individual's computer. As more communications are facilitated through these cloud-based programs, it is no surprise that government and law enforcement would seek to access

---

* This is an edited, reformatted and augmented version of a Congressional Research Service publication, CRS Report for Congress R43015, from www.crs.gov, prepared for Members and Committees of Congress, dated March 22, 2013.

this stored information to conduct criminal investigations, prevent cyber threats, and thwart terrorist attacks, among other purposes. This prompts the following questions: (1) What legal protections are in place for information shared and stored in the cloud? (2) What legal process must the government follow to obtain this information? and (3) How do these rules differ from those applied in the physical world?

Protections of communications in the physical world flow from the Fourth Amendment and various federal statutes such as the Electronic Communications Privacy Act of 1986 (ECPA), which includes the Stored Communications Act (SCA). Under the Fourth Amendment, government officials are generally prohibited from accessing an individual's communication, such as tapping into a telephone call or opening a postal letter, without first obtaining judicial approval. In the digital world, courts have by and large required law enforcement to acquire a warrant before accessing the contents of electronic communications, but have permitted law enforcement to access non-content information such as routing data with lesser process. These cases do not seem to distinguish between cloud-based and traditional forms of Internet services.

Federal courts have applied the SCA to various electronic communications including e-mails, messages sent on social networking sites like Facebook and MySpace, and movies posted on video-sharing sites like YouTube. The process for obtaining these communications under the SCA depends on how long the information has been stored with the service provider and how the provider is classified under the SCA. The relatively few cases dealing with cloud computing have required lesser legal process for accessing electronic communications sent via cloud-based services than traditional forms of Internet computing.

In light of this rapidly changing technology, there have been several legislative proposals to augment the Fourth Amendment's protections for digital communications and update existing statutory protections like the SCA for information shared and stored in the cloud.

INTRODUCTION

Although it is difficult to provide a precise definition of "cloud computing," it is generally described as web-based services that allow users to access anything from e-mail to social media to banking to more complex programs like business computing.[1] Traditionally, users would download software and manipulate data on their own computer, while in the cloud, this activity occurs over the Internet on a third-party computer. Many e-mail services like Gmail and Hotmail operate using cloud computing, as do music programs like Grooveshark and Pandora, and social media sites like Facebook and Twitter.[2] Likewise, many smartphone applications employ cloud computing that permits users to store and access large amounts of data. Cloud storage is also on the rise, with an estimated 500 million users by year end, and 1.3 billion users by 2017.[3] Cloud storage services like DropBox, Google Drive, and SkyDrive by Microsoft allow users to store their information on the computer of a third-party and access it from any platform with Internet access.[4]

As cloud computing becomes integrated into our daily lives, a host of personal information (e.g., private communications, financial data, photographs, etc.) will be stored on a server owned by a third party. This raises privacy and security issues, including when and how government may access this information as part of a criminal or other type of investigation. This report first describes cloud computing and how it differs from traditional computing. It then describes how the Fourth Amendment and federal electronic privacy statutes apply to communications in the physical world, to Internet communications generally, and specifically to the cloud. Finally, this report surveys recent legislation and other various proposals designed to update the existing statutory framework.

PRIVACY FOR COMMUNICATIONS IN THE PHYSICAL WORLD

Because many traditional activities are increasingly being transferred online, it is vital to first understand what privacy protections apply in the physical world before turning to possible protections in the cloud. The Fourth Amendment and federal communication statutes provide the core privacy protections in the physical world.

The Fourth Amendment provides, in relevant part, that "[t]he right of the people to be secure in their persons, houses, papers, and effects, against unreasonable searches and seizures, shall not be violated[.]"[5] The primary purpose of the Fourth Amendment is to ensure the privacy of the citizenry and to prevent arbitrary government intrusion into their lives. To determine if the Fourth Amendment applies in a given case, a court tests whether the government activities constitute a *search*. The modern formulation for determining whether certain conduct is a search under the Fourth Amendment derives from Justice Harlan's concurrence in *Katz v. United States*.[6] This test asks "first that a person have exhibited an actual (subjective) expectation of privacy and, second, that the expectation be one that society is prepared to recognize as 'reasonable.'"[7] What is *reasonable* in a given case—the yardstick for all Fourth Amendment analyses—can depend greatly on the facts of the case.[8] However, there are certain lines of cases that provide baseline rules for the protection of communications in the physical world.

The closest analog to an e-mail in the physical world is the postal letter. In 1878, the Supreme Court was asked to rule in *Ex parte Jackson* whether Congress had the constitutional authority to exclude certain obscene material from the United States' postal system.[9] In discussing the nature of protecting the postal system, the Court observed that:

> Letters and sealed packages of this kind in the mail are as fully guarded from examination and inspection, except as to their outward form and weight, as if they were retained by the parties forwarding them in their own domiciles. The constitutional guaranty of the right of the people to be secure in their papers against unreasonable searches and seizures extends to their papers, thus closed against inspection, wherever they may be. Whilst in the mail, they can only be opened and examined under like warrant, issued upon similar oath or affirmation, particularly describing the thing to be seized, as is required when papers are subjected to search in one's own household. No law of Congress can place in the hands of officials connected with the postal service any authority to invade the secrecy of letters and such sealed packages in the mail; and all regulations adopted as to mail matter of this kind must be in subordination to the great principle embodied in the fourth amendment of the Constitution.[10]

The Court in *Ex parte Jackson* relied on a content/non-content distinction to find that the inside of the letter (the content) was protected, while the routing information on the outside (non-content) was not subject to similar Fourth Amendment restrictions.

Of more recent vintage, the Court observed in *United States v. Jacobsen* that "[l]etters and other sealed packages are in the general class of effects in which the public at large has a legitimate expectation of privacy; warrantless searches of such effects are presumptively unreasonable."[11] The free flow of mail, however, is not absolute. In *United States v. Leeuwen*, the Court held that government officials may detain packages for a brief period of time without a warrant to confirm the suspicious nature of the package.[12] Additionally, under federal regulations postal workers can record the outside, routing information on letters sent, a technique known as a mail cover, to gather evidence regarding the commission of a crime.[13] These same regulations, however, prohibit postal employees from opening the mail, unless one of the limited exceptions applies.[14]

Like the contents of letters, the contents of a conversation—the words spoken either in person or through a device such as a cell phone or land-line phone—are generally protected under various constitutional and federal statutory provisions. In *United States v. Katz*, the Court held that the contents of an individual's conversation are protected under the Fourth Amendment, even when spoken in a public telephone booth.[15] The Court remarked that an individual who makes a telephone call from a closed telephone booth "is surely entitled to assume that the words he utters into the mouthpiece will not be broadcast to the world. To read the Constitution more narrowly is to ignore the vital role that the public telephone has come to play in private communication."[16] Congress augmented *Katz* in Title III of the Omnibus Crime Control and Safe Streets Act of 1968[17] as amended by the Electronic Communications Privacy Act of 1986 (ECPA),[18] establishing significant restrictions on surreptitious interception of private communications. Commonly referred to as the Wiretap Act, Title III prohibits the intentional interception of telephone, face-to-face, and electronic communications using a mechanical or other device, unless one of several exceptions applies, such as consent of one of the parties to the conversation, or a judicially authorized warrant based upon probable cause.[19]

Although accessing the contents of a telephone communication generally requires a probable cause warrant, access to telephone routing information, including the numbers dialed, requires lesser process. In *Smith v. Maryland*, the Court applied the third-party doctrine to the telephone numbers a person dials to place a call.[20] The third-party doctrine provides that information a person voluntarily conveys to another person is generally not protected by the Fourth Amendment.[21] The Court observed in *Smith* that when the defendant used his phone, he "voluntarily conveyed numerical information to the telephone company and 'exposed' that information to its equipment in the ordinary course of business. In so doing, [he] assumed the risk that the company would reveal to police the numbers he dialed."[22] Seven years later, Congress included in ECPA a prohibition against the use of pen registers and trap and trace devices (which can record the incoming and outgoing telephone numbers from a certain customer), unless the government obtained a court order certifying that the information to be obtained is "relevant to an ongoing criminal investigation."[23]

Another crucial form of communication in the modern world that is increasingly moving to the cloud is the transfer of business records. In *United States v. Miller*, the Court applied the third-party doctrine to hold that a bank customer has no legitimate expectation of privacy in banking documents such as checks and deposit slips transferred to a bank in the ordinary course of business.[24] There, the Court observed that "[t]he depositor takes the risk, in revealing his affairs to another, that the information will be conveyed by that person to the government. ... This Court has held repeatedly that the Fourth Amendment does not prohibit the obtaining of information revealed to a third party and conveyed by him to Government authorities, even if the information is revealed on the assumption that it will be used only for a limited purpose and the confidence placed in the third party will not be betrayed."[25] In reaction to *Miller*, Congress enacted the Right to Financial Privacy Act, creating a statutory protection for these financial documents.[26]

PRIVACY FOR COMMUNICATIONS ON THE INTERNET

Although the jurisprudence of Internet privacy is in its infancy, the current body of case law sheds light on how the Fourth Amendment and federal statutes apply to the cloud. When applying the Fourth Amendment, it appears that courts have not distinguished between traditional forms of Internet communication and cloud-based communication; the same rules apply to each. However, when applying the Stored Communications Act, cloud computing such as web-based e-mails or messaging through social network sites has not received the robust privacy protections accorded to traditional e-mail services.

Fourth Amendment

For the most part, courts have applied the Fourth Amendment to Internet communications by analogy to the physical world.[27] Like the traditional cases, the outcomes of the Internet cases have hinged on whether the information sought by the government was considered "content" or "noncontent."[28] Generally, the courts have held that access to Internet communications that constitute the content of the communication is a search for which a warrant is required. By contrast, access to information that reveals only non-content information such as routing information—including an Internet Protocol address (IP address) or the to/from address in an e-mail—has been subjected to lesser legal process.

In 2007, the Ninth Circuit Court of Appeals held in *Forrester v. United States* that the government's access to the "non-content" information transferred as part of an Internet communication—such as the to/from address line in an e-mail—did not constitute a search under the Fourth Amendment.[29] In that case, several defendants were allegedly manufacturing ecstasy in violation of federal drug laws. During its investigation, the government sought to intercept defendant Dennis Alba's Internet and e-mail activity. The government received a court order to install a "mirror port" at Alba's Internet service provider, which enabled the government to learn the to/from addresses of his e-mails, the IP addresses of the websites he visited, and the total volume of information sent to or from his account. At trial, Alba claimed that this evidence was obtained in violation of his Fourth Amendment right to be free from unreasonable searches and seizures. In denying Alba's claim, the Ninth Circuit relied on two lines of Fourth Amendment cases. First, the court analogized this routing information to the telephone numbers dialed in the third-party case, *Smith v. Maryland.*[30] Like the defendant in *Smith* who should have expected the numbers he dialed would be revealed to the carrier that would place his call, "e-mail and internet users have no expectation of privacy in the to/from addresses of their messages or the IP addresses of the websites they visit because they should know that this information is provided to and used by the service provider for the specific purpose of directing and routing of information."[31] Second, the panel likened the addressing information of electronic communications to the outside address information on physical mail, which is generally not protected under the Fourth Amendment.[32] Because e-mails contain similar addressing information, the court concluded that they are not entitled to Fourth Amendment safeguards.

Like *Forrester*, the Third Circuit Court of Appeals in *United States v. Christie* held that individuals do not have a reasonable expectation of privacy in their IP addresses.[33] This case originated when the FBI acquired the IP addresses of computer users who were accessing child pornography websites. The FBI then requested the names of the users linked to these IP addresses from their ISP. Again, applying the third-party doctrine, the court held that "no reasonable expectation of privacy exists in an IP address, because that information is also conveyed to and, indeed, from third parties, including ISPs. IP addresses are not merely passively conveyed through third party equipment, but rather are voluntarily turned over in order to direct the third party's servers."[34]

Although the panel in *Forrester* concluded that outside address information that is visible to a third-party carrier is not subject to Fourth Amendment protection, it commented in passing that "the *contents* may deserve Fourth Amendment protection" and that certain surveillance techniques may "breach the line between mere addressing and more content-rich information."[35]

In 2010, the Sixth Circuit Court of Appeals in *United States v. Warshak* recognized this difference between content and non-content information, holding that the content of e-mail communications is protected under the Fourth Amendment.[36] There, Warshak was being investigated for a scheme to defraud customers of his company. The government sought and obtained permission from Warshak's ISP to preserve the contents of Warshak's e-mails, and eventually the government was permitted access to approximately 27,000 e-mails. Warshak then moved to suppress this access as forbidden under the Fourth Amendment absent a warrant. The Sixth Circuit held that the contents of the e-mails were protected under the Fourth Amendment. Like the Ninth Circuit decision, the ruling in *Warshak* compared e-mails to physical mail, observing that "[g]iven the fundamental similarities between e-mail and traditional forms of communication, it would defy common sense to afford e-mails lesser Fourth Amendment protection."[37] The panel noted the importance of email as an "indispensable part" of modern society.[38] The panel held that "if government agents compel an ISP to surrender the contents of a subscriber's e-mails, those agents have thereby conducted a Fourth Amendment search, which necessitates compliance with the warrant requirement absent some exception."[39]

Thus, while slim, this body of case law applying the Fourth Amendment to Internet communications seems to establish several rules. First, for government officials to access the contents of e-mails or other electronic communications, they must obtain a warrant based upon probable cause absent a warrant exception. Second, if the government seeks non-content information such as subscriber information, the to/from line on an e-mail, or the IP addresses of websites visited, a subpoena will generally suffice. Additionally, it does not appear that these courts consider the nature of the e-mail service provided, whether cloud-based or the traditional client-based e-mail, as part of their Fourth Amendment analysis. It would seem that these same rules apply to both types of services.

Stored Communications Act (SCA)

In the early 1980s, Congress voiced concern that electronic communications were not accorded the same privacy as analogous communications in the physical world. The Senate Judiciary Committee observed in 1986 that "[p]rivacy cannot be left to depend solely on physical protection, or it will gradually erode as technology advances."[40] Likewise, the House Judiciary Committee noted other problems with unclear legal standards relating to access to electronic communications.[41] The House Committee feared that unclear legal standards would discourage potential customers from using this new technology. The House Committee was also concerned that police officers who were conducting investigations may face liability or that evidence obtained may not be admissible in a criminal prosecution.[42] In light of these concerns, Congress overhauled federal communication privacy laws in 1986 as part of the Electronic

Communications Privacy Act of 1986 (ECPA).[43] The Stored Communications Act (SCA), enacted as Title II of ECPA, was designed to regulate the access and dissemination of electronic communications stored on computers. The SCA has two core components: (1) the procedures the government must follow to compel disclosure of stored communications;[44] and (2) the situations in which a service provider may voluntarily share a customer's communications.[45]

Scope of the SCA

The SCA covers providers of two types of public services: an "electronic communication service," or ECS, and a "remote computing service," or RCS. An ECS provider is any service which allows its customers to "send or receive wire or electronic communications."[46] An ECS provider is prohibited from "knowingly divulg[ing] to any person or entity the contents of a communication while in electronic storage by that service[,]" subject to certain exceptions.[47] "Electronic storage" is in turn defined as information that is stored (1) incidental to the transmission of that communication, or (2) for backup purposes.[48] An RCS provider is defined as "the provision to the public of computer storage or processing services by means of an electronic communications system[.]" An RCS is prohibited, also subject to certain exceptions, from "knowingly divulg[ing] to any person or entity the contents of any communication which is carried or maintained on that service."[49]

Required Disclosure of Communications

Section 2703 of the SCA sets forth the procedures the government must follow to gain access to electronic communications, such as e-mails, from an ECS or RCS provider. Section 2703 is tiered—the more content-rich the information sought, the higher the level of evidentiary proof the government must proffer.

At the highest level, § 2703(a) requires the government to obtain a warrant if it seeks access to the *content* of a communication from an ECS provider that has been in "electronic storage" for 180 days or less.[50] The same procedure is available for communications stored for *more* than 180 days from an ECS provider or from an RCS provider (no matter how long the communication is stored with it), but there are two other alternatives. If the government provides notice to the customer, it can access these older communications with a subpoena or a court order under § 2703(d).[51] These § 2703(d) orders require the applicant to prove "specific and articulable facts, showing that there are reasonable grounds to believe that the contents of a[n] ... electronic communication ... are relevant and material to an ongoing criminal investigation."[52]

In addition to the content of communications, the SCA permits access to non-content information with a warrant, but the government may use a subpoena or a § 2703(d) order without having to provide the customer notice.[53] To access subscriber information, including the customer's name, address, phone number, length of service, and means of payment (including bank account numbers), the government may follow the more stringent requirements for obtaining a warrant or a § 2703(d) order, but can also use an administrative subpoena, which requires no prior authorization by a judicial officer.[54]

Voluntary Disclosure of Communications

Section 2702 establishes when a service provider may voluntarily disclose the content of communications and customer information to another entity. This section applies only to service providers to the "public";[55] thus, non-public providers can turn over these documents without any process required.[56] For public providers, the contents of a communication may not be divulged unless one of the eight exceptions in § 2702(b) applies, which include consent of one of the parties to the communication; as a necessary incident to the rendition of services; in connection with a missing child; inadvertently obtained and pertains to the commission of a crime; or if there is imminent risk of death or serious physical injury to any person.[57] A public provider may release customers' records or other non-content information if it meets one of the six exceptions provided in § 2702(c), which include consent of the subscriber; as a necessary incident to the rendition of services; and in connection with a missing child.[58]

Application of the SCA E-mails

It is clear from the text of the SCA that government access to the content of *unopened* e-mails stored for 180 days or less by an electronic communication service requires a warrant.[59] It is also clear that opened or unopened e-mails stored for more than 180 days may be accessed with a subpoena or a § 2703(d) order, so long as the government provides notice to the subscriber.[60] However, there is a split in the courts as to whether an *opened* e-mail stored 180 days or less is in "electronic storage" under the SCA. The practical result of this definitional breakdown is that police must get a warrant if the communication is in electronic storage, but need only use a subpoena if not. One of the substantial points of departure is how these divided courts view the difference between traditional forms of e-mail such as client-based services and web-based e-mails that rely on cloud technology.

In *Theofel v. Farey-Jones* before the Ninth Circuit Court of Appeals, the defendant Farey-Jones subpoenaed the plaintiffs' ISP provider NetGate for access to "[a]ll copies of e-mails sent or received by anyone" within the plaintiff's company.[61] NetGate provided some, but not all of the e-mails. The plaintiffs sued Farey-Jones under, among other statutes, § 2701 of the Stored Communications Act, for unlawful access to their e-mail communications. The crux of this issue was whether the e-mails were in "electronic storage" under the SCA.[62] Again, "electronic storage" is defined as "(A) any temporary, intermediate storage of a wire or electronic communication incidental to the electronic transmission thereof; and (B) any storage of such communication by an electronic communication service for purposes of backup protection of such communication.... "[63] If they were in electronic storage, the subpoena used would be insufficient to access the e-mails. The court held that these e-mails were for backup purposes under subsection (B), and observed:

> An obvious purpose for storing a message on an ISP's server after delivery is to provide a second copy of the message in the event that the user needs to download it again-if, for example, the message is accidentally erased from the user's own computer. The ISP copy of the message functions as a "backup" for the user. Notably, nothing in the Act requires that the backup protection be for the benefit of the

> ISP rather than the user. Storage under these circumstances thus literally falls within the statutory definition.[64]

The Ninth Circuit concluded that "where the underlying message has expired in the normal course, any copy is no longer performing any backup function."[65] *Theofel*'s holding appears to apply when the user downloads a message on his computer and the ISP keeps a copy of the e-mail for "backup protection." However, it is uncertain whether a future court would apply this rule to cloud computing where the only copy of the message is left on the service provider's computer. In passing, the Ninth Circuit noted that "[a] remote computing service might be the only place a user stores his messages; in that case, the messages are not stored for backup purposes."[66] The court seems to be stating that this rule would not apply to some e-mail providers—possibly cloud providers. One observer has suggested that this dicta in *Theofel* evidences that e-mails stored in the cloud would not be stored for backup purposes, and thus, would not be subject to the more stringent warrant requirement.[67] The District Court for the Central District of Illinois picked up on this distinction in *United States v. Weaver,* where it had to apply the SCA to a cloud-based e-mail system. There, the government sought e-mails from Justin Weaver's Microsoft Hotmail account as part of its child pornography investigation.[68] The government executed a subpoena to Microsoft seeking any opened or sent email from Weaver's account. Microsoft produced some e-mails to the government, but failed to produce e-mails that had already been opened and those that had been stored for fewer than 181 days. The court had to determine whether these e-mails were in "electronic storage" under § 2703(a), as defined in § 2510(17), or "storage" under § 2703(b)(2).[69] If they were in "electronic storage" then the government should have produced a warrant to access them; if they were not, the subpoena would suffice.

Noting that the e-mails sought by the government were those already opened, the court concluded that they were not in "temporary, intermediate storage" under subsection (A) of § 2510(17). Turning to subsection (B), the court had to determine if they were being stored for "backup protection." Reviewing the nature of web-based e-mail, which relies on cloud technology, the court observed that "Hotmail users can access their e-mail over the web from any computer, and they do not automatically download their messages to their own computers as non-web-based email service users do. Instead, if Hotmail users save a message, they generally leave it on the Hotmail server and return to Hotmail via the web to access it on subsequent occasions."[70] The court went to say that the result may differ if the "users opt to connect an e-mail program, such as Microsoft Outlook" to their e-mail accounts and download messages to their own computers. However, the court concluded that if someone uses a pure cloud-based e-mail system, those e-mails cannot be stored for "backup purposes" under subsection (B) as they would be the only copy of the e-mails. Once the user opened the e-mail and left it on the Hotmail account, Microsoft was "maintaining the messages 'solely for the purpose of providing storage or computer processing services to such subscriber or customer.'"[71] This made Microsoft an RCS, rather than an ECS provider. Thus, the e-mails were subject only to the subpoena requirement.

Social Networking

In *Crispin v. Christian Audigier, Inc.*, the United States District Court for the Central District of California was asked whether messages sent through private messaging services or through posting on user-created profile pages on social networking sites Facebook and MySpace are covered under the SCA.[72] *Crispin* arose as part of discovery requests in private litigation, when defendant Christian Audigier served subpoenas on Facebook and MySpace for access to communications between the plaintiff and a third party. The plaintiff moved to quash the subpoenas, arguing that Facebook and MySpace were prohibited from disclosing the communication under § 2702(a)(1) of the SCA.[73] As to the private messages sent on these social networking sites, the court relied on *Weaver* and the dicta in *Theofel* to hold that when messages are opened and retained on the site, Facebook and MySpace operate as RCS providers, and the messages are subject only to the subpoena requirement.[74]

The court next turned to the "wall postings" on Facebook and the MySpace comments page, which permit users to post messages on another user's profile space. The court first analogized these comment pages to the traditional electronic bulletin board services (BBS). A BBS is a website that permits users to post messages on a "board" for the general public to view. Precedent and legislative history established that these bulletin boards were covered under the SCA.[75] However, to be entitled to protection under the SCA, access to messages posted on these sites must be restricted in some meaningful way from the public at large.[76] Facebook and MySpace, the court reasoned, provide a similar function: they permit users to post messages on other users' "walls" so long as they have authorization to do so.[77] Although these social networking sites were considered ECSs, the court still had to determine whether the information had been in "electronic storage" under the SCA. The court concluded that messages that had not been retrieved fell within the first definition of electronic storage—that is, that they were being temporarily stored "incidental to transmission." However, because Crispin had already accessed the messages, they fell within the second electronic storage pathway—stored for backup purposes.[78] Ultimately, the Court remanded the case to the magistrate judge to determine if "either the general public had access to plaintiff's Facebook and MySpace comments, or access was limited to a few."[79] If the latter, the communications would fall under the SCA's protections and the subpoena would be quashed.

YouTube Videos

In *Viacom Intern. Inc. v. YouTube Inc.*, the federal district court for the Southern District of New York had to determine whether access to YouTube videos was governed by the SCA.[80] There, Viacom claimed that videos posted on Google's video-sharing website YouTube violated federal copyright law. Viacom requested certain videos from Google as part of its discovery requests. The court first concluded, with little discussion, that Google was an RCS provider under the SCA.[81] It then moved on to the question of whether the SCA permitted such disclosure. Viacom argued that users who posted videos on YouTube have authorized disclosure of those videos under § 2702(b)(3), which allows the provider to "divulge the contents of a communication ... with the lawful consent of ... the subscriber."[82] The court rejected this argument, observing that, although YouTube's Terms of Use and Privacy Policy provides a disclaimer that any video posted in the public areas of the site may be divulged, none of the provisions in that user agreement "can be fairly construed as a grant of permission from users to reveal to plaintiffs the videos they have designated as private and chosen to share only with specified recipients."[83] Thus, the court held the SCA did not permit Viacom access to those videos that had been marked private by the user who posted them.[84] The court, however, permitted Viacom access to non-content data such as "the number of times each video has been viewed on YouTube.com or made accessible on a third-party website through an 'embedded' link to the video."[85]

DIFFERENCES IN PRIVACY PROTECTIONS IN THE PHYSICAL WORLD, TRADITIONAL COMPUTING, AND CLOUD COMPUTING

In summary, there are many similarities between searches in the physical and digital worlds. For instance, for law enforcement to access the contents of a postal letter, it must first obtain a warrant based upon probable cause, but routing information on the outside of the letter does not receive the same protection.[86]

This distinction also applies to telephone calls, where law enforcement cannot surreptitiously record the content of one's conversation, but can access the numbers dialed with lesser process.[87] The limited number of courts reviewing this issue under the Fourth Amendment have applied this same content/non-content distinction to electronic communications such as e-mails. To access the content of an e-mail, law enforcement generally must obtain a warrant. To obtain the routing information, such as an IP address or the to/from address of an e-mail, a subpoena will usually suffice.

However, there are also differences between searches in the physical world and the Internet. For example, under the SCA, the government can access the contents of e-mails stored for more than 180 days, and in some circuits, e-mails that have been opened no matter how long they are stored, with a subpoena and notice to the customer.

This is a clear difference from the physical world, as the government cannot access one's private physical letters, no matter how long they are stored, without a warrant.

Also, in many instances, evidence obtained by an illegal search in the physical world is not admissible in a criminal prosecution under the exclusionary rule.

Under the SCA, however, there is no suppression remedy; thus, even evidence unlawfully obtained may be admitted into evidence at trial.[88] In any event, if applicable, the Fourth Amendment provides a baseline threshold which the SCA cannot lessen.[89]

Additionally, the few courts that applied the SCA to e-mail and other Internet communications seem to have created a dividing line between traditional forms of Internet computing and cloud-based computing. For instance, under the Ninth Circuit's approach in *Theofel,* traditional e-mail services are covered under the SCA's more stringent warrant requirement, whereas the cloud-based e-mails in *Weaver* were subject to the lesser subpoena requirement.

In *Viacom Intern. Inc.*, Youtube was considered an RCS provider thus also subjecting posted videos to the subpoena requirement. It remains to be seen whether future courts will apply this distinction between cloud-based and traditional forms of electronic communications.

PROPOSED CHANGES TO THE CURRENT STATUTORY FRAMEWORK

Several courts, commentators, and government officials alike have called for an overhaul of ECPA, though disagreement may exist as to how to balance the competing interests of the government, the communications industry, and the individual.

Senator Patrick J. Leahy, chairman of the Senate Judiciary Committee, observed at a committee hearing that while ECPA is a useful tool for government officials, it is "hampered by conflicting standards that cause confusion for law enforcement, the business community, and American consumers alike."[90]

He further observed that "a single e-mail could be subject to as many as four different levels of privacy protections under ECPA, depending on where it is stored and when it is sent."[91]

Several observers have also opined on perceived flaws in the SCA: "It is more complicated than it needs to be. It has sections that are redundant and merely confusing.

The absence of a statutory suppression remedy has created significant uncertainty about how the statute works.

The SCA also offers surprisingly low privacy protections when the government seeks to compel the contents other than unretrieved communications held pending transmission for 180 days or less."[92] The Department of Justice has also called for changes to ECPA, but has cautioned against the implementation of a heightened standard for accessing electronic communications:

> Congress may wish to consider that raising the standard for obtaining information under ECPA may substantially slow criminal and national security investigations. In general, it takes longer for law enforcement to prepare a 2703(d) order application than a subpoena, and it takes longer to obtain a search warrant than a 2703(d) order. In a wide range of investigations, including terrorism, violent crimes, and child exploitation, speed is often judged to be essential.[93]

Legislation has been introduced in the 112th and 113th Congresses, and various measures have been proposed by other entities, to overhaul ECPA.

Recent Legislative Proposals

Recent legislative proposals introduced in the 112th and 113th Congresses aim to clarify and strengthen the requirements for accessing an individual's electronic communications under the SCA. [94] Although the language in each bill differs, several of the provisions in each bill relating to the SCA have the same substantive effect. These bills would:

- require a government entity to obtain a warrant based upon probable cause to retrieve the content of information from both providers of electronic communication services and remote computing services;
- eliminate the 180-day rule currently contained in § 2703(a), so that communications stored for 180 days or 181 days would be treated the same;
- amend § 2703(a) to not only cover communications in "electronic storage" but also those that are being "held or maintained" by that service;
- require the government to notify the customer of any search conducted under the SCA within three days, including a copy of the warrant, unless delayed notice is permitted under § 2705; and
- eliminate the ability of providers to voluntarily share content and subscriber information with a government entity unless one of the § 2702(b) exceptions applies.

Additionally, H.R. 6399 from the 112th Congress would have also:

- created a statutory suppression remedy for violations of the SCA;[95]
- required the Administrative Office of the United States Courts to report annually to Congress on how many orders or warrants were sought and issued concerning the contents of electronic communications; and
- required a provider to report annually to the Administrative Office of the United States Courts the number of legal demands it has received from federal, state, and local law enforcement agencies, and the number of accounts about which information was disclosed. The providers can receive compensation for the costs of compiling these records.

Other Proposals

Uniformity and Technology Neutrality

Although each of the legislative proposals above would apply the same rules to both ECS and RCS providers, it is not clear that this approach would sufficiently capture all of the various communications that occur in the cloud. As some observers have pointed out, sites such as eBay, which permit users to buy and sell items online, are probably not ECS providers, as they do not provide users the ability to send or receive communications on the Internet.[96] And it has been argued that the site is not an RCS provider, as it does not provide "processing service" for its users, although he notes this debate is ambiguous at best as this term is neither defined by statute nor construed in any case.

Thus, even if Congress applies the same rules to both ECS and RCS providers, some cloud services such as eBay might still not be covered. Congress could either draft language specifically covering cloud services, or draft a broad definition for the class of entities that would come within the SCA's ambit, preferably aiming for technology neutrality.

Another observer offered the following language, which intends to rescind the 180-day rule, apply the same rules to all service providers, and provide protections even if a message has been received or downloaded by the user:

> A governmental entity may only require a provider of communications services to disclose the contents of a wire or electronic communication, if transmitted or stored electronically, only upon the issuance of a warrant by a court of competent jurisdiction, whether or not the provider stores the communication after receipt by the user, and regardless of whether the communication remains on the server after receipt or is downloaded to the user's device.[97]

Consent Provisions

Currently, there is an exception under ECPA for interceptions made with prior consent of one of the parties to the communication.[98] However, ECPA does not define "consent." For instance, does clicking on a user agreement when one signs up for Gmail or Hotmail suffice as consent for these providers to access the content of one's e-mails and share them with the government? One commentator has suggested that the consent requirement should be clarified:

> Notably, an e-mail service might scan the contents of customers' e-mail messages for content that suggests an interest in certain products and may provide that information to behavioral advertising agencies that create consumer databases and feed online ads on behalf of their clients. Under ECPA, those service providers have violated the law if they have not obtained user consent for those practices. Unfortunately, ECPA's failure to define consent leaves users and service providers without guidance on this point. Is a consumer's decision to use a monitored e-mail service, after being given an opportunity to read a privacy policy, sufficient to indicate consent? Or should explicit opt-in consent, pursuant to conspicuous notice, be required?[99]

As an example of this opt-in regime, as part of the Driver's Privacy Protection Act, Congress required state motor vehicle departments to receive the express consent of individuals before sharing certain personal information.[100] A similar approach could be implemented with ECPA.

CONCLUSION

The Supreme Court once remarked that when an individual "puts something in his filing cabinet, in his desk drawer, or in his pocket, he has the right to know it will be secure from an unreasonable search or an unreasonable seizure."[101] Does this proposition hold true today when people turn to digital desk drawers, digital filing cabinets, and digital pockets? For the most part, many of the protections that apply to the physical world have been transferred to the digital world. In the physical world the contents of letters, telephone calls, and other forms of communication are generally protected by the Fourth Amendment's prohibition against unreasonable searches and seizures. The limited number of courts reviewing the question have held that the content of Internet communications are similarly protected from government searches under the Fourth Amendment. These protections may be supplemented by the SCA, which accords varying degrees of privacy safeguards to both public and private intrusions, depending on how long the communication has been stored and how the provider of the network service is classified under its complicated definitions. Additionally, courts have occasionally applied lesser degrees of protection to communications sent and received through cloud-based services than with traditional forms of Internet communications, based on the manner the information is stored by each, and how such storage is defined under the

SCA. Recent legislative proposals would apply the same rules to communications in the physical and digital worlds and between traditional computing and cloud computing.

End Notes

[1] Jonathan Strickland, How Cloud Computing Works, HOW STUFF WORKS (last visited Oct. 15, 2012), http://computer.howstuffworks.com/cloud-computing/cloud-computing.htm /printable. The National Institute of Standards and Technology defines cloud computing as "a model for enabling ubiquitous, convenient, on-demand network access to a shared pool of configurable computing resources (e.g., networks, servers, storage, applications, and services) that can be rapidly provisioned and released with minimal management effort or service provider interaction." NAT'L INST. STANDARDS & TECH., THE NIST DEFINITION OF CLOUD COMPUTING, Spec. Pub. 800-145, at 2 (2011), available at http://csrc.nist.gov/publications/nistpubs/800-145/SP800-145.pdf.

[2] Rivka Tadjer, What is Cloud Computing?, PC MAGAZINE (Nov. 18, 2010), http://www. pcmag.com/article2/ 0,2817,2372165,00.asp.

[3] Jagdish Rebello, Consumers Aggressively Migrate Data to Cloud Storage in the First Half of 2012, IHS ISUPPLI (Oct. 15, 2012), http://www.isuppli.com/Mobile-and-Wireless-Communications/News/Pages/Consumers-AggressivelyMigrate-Data-to-Cloud-Storage-in-First-Half-of-2012.aspx.

[4] Jonathan Strickland, How Cloud Computing Works, HOW STUFF WORKS (last visited Oct. 15, 2015), available at http://computer.howstuffworks.com/cloud-computing/cloud-storage.htm.

[5] U.S. CONST. amend. IV.

[6] Katz v. United States, 389 U.S. 347, 361 (1967) (Harlan, J., concurring).

[7] Id.

[8] Brigham City v. Stuart, 547 U.S. 398, 403 (2006) ("[T]he ultimate touchstone of the Fourth Amendment is 'reasonableness.'").

[9] Ex parte Jackson, 96 U.S. 727 (1877).

[10] Id. at 733.

[11] United States v. Jacobsen, 466 U.S. 109, 115 (1984).

[12] United States v. Leeuwen, 397 U.S. 249, 253 (1970) ("No interest protected by the Fourth Amendment was invaded by forwarding the packages the following day rather than the day when they were deposited. The significant Fourth Amendment interest was in the privacy of this first-class mail; and that privacy was not disturbed or invaded until the approval of the magistrate was obtained.").

[13] 39 C.F.R. § 233.3(a). Several federal circuit courts have upheld the mail cover practice under the Fourth Amendment. See United States v. Choate, 576 F.2d 165 (9th Cir. 1978); United States v. Huie, 593 F.2d 14 (5th Cir. 1979).

[14] 39 C.F.R. § 233.3(g) ("No person in the Postal Service except those employed for that purpose in dead-mail offices, may open, or inspect the contents of, or permit the opening or inspection of sealed mail without a federal search warrant, even though it may contain criminal or otherwise nonmailable matter, or furnish evidence of the commission of a crime, or the violation of a postal statute.").

[15] Katz v. United States, 389 U.S. 347, 359 (1967).
[16] Id. at 352.
[17] Omnibus Crime Control and Safe Streets Act of 1968, P.L. 90-351, § 801, 82 Stat. 197, 211.
[18] Electronic Communications Privacy Act of 1986, P.L. 99-508, § 101, 100 Stat. 1848, 1848.
[19] 18 U.S.C. § 2511(1). See generally CRS Report 98-326, Privacy: An Overview of Federal Statutes Governing Wiretapping and Electronic Eavesdropping, by Gina Stevens and Charles Doyle.
[20] Smith v. Maryland, 442 U.S. 735 (1979).
[21] The same theory applies when one party to a conversation records or discloses it. United States v. White, 401 U.S. 745 (1971).
[22] Id. at 744.
[23] 18 U.S.C. § 3123(a)(1).
[24] United States v. Miller, 425 U.S. 435, 443 (1976).
[25] Id.
[26] Right to Financial Privacy Act of 1978, P.L. 95-630, 92 Stat. 3697 (codified at 12 U.S.C. §§ 3401-3422).
[27] See David A. Couillard, Defogging the Cloud: Applying the Fourth Amendment Principles to Evolving Privacy Expectations in Cloud Computing, 93 MINN. L. REV. 2205, 2219 (2009).
[28] See Orin Kerr, Applying the Fourth Amendment to the Internet: A General Approach, 62 STAN. L. REV. 1005, 1029 (2010).
[29] United States v. Forrester, 512 F.3d 500, 509 (9th Cir. 2007).
[30] Smith v. Maryland, 442 U.S. 735 (1979).
[31] Forrester, 512 F.3d at 510.
[32] See Ex Parte Jackson, 96 U.S. 727, 732 (1878).
[33] United States v. Christie, 624 F.3d 558, 574 (3d Cir. 2010).
[34] Christie, 624 F.3d at 574 (internal quotation marks omitted). Court have also held that individuals do not have a reasonable expectation of privacy in their subscriber information. See, e.g., Guest v. Leis, 255 F.3d 325, 336 (6th Cir. 2001) ("We conclude that plaintiffs in these cases lack a Fourth Amendment privacy interest in their subscriber information because they communicated it to the systems operators."); United States v. Bynum, 604 F.3d 161, 164 (4th Cir. 2010) ("[The defendant] can point to no evidence that he had a subjective expectation of privacy in his internet and phone 'subscriber information'—i.e., his name, e-mail address, telephone number, and physical address—which the Government obtained through the administrative subpoenas. Bynum voluntarily conveyed all this information to his internet and phone companies. In so doing, [the defendant] 'assumed the risk that th[os]e compan[ies] would reveal [that information] to police.'"); United States v. Perrine, 518 F.3d 1196, 1204 (10th Cir. 2008) (same).
[35] Forrester, 512 F.3d at 511 (emphasis added).
[36] United States v. Warshak, 631 F.3d 266 (6th Cir. 2010).
[37] Id. at 286 ("E-mail is the technological scion of tangible mail, and it plays an indispensable part in the Information Age. ... As some forms of communication begin to diminish, the Fourth Amendment must recognize and protect nascent ones that arise.")
[38] Id.
[39] Id.
[40] S.Rept. 99-541, at 5 (1986).
[41] H.Rept. 99-647, at 19 (1986).
[42] Id.

[43] Electronic Communications Privacy Act of 1986, P.L. 99-508, 100 Stat. 1848.

[44] 18 U.S.C. § 2703.

[45] 18 U.S.C. § 2702.

[46] 18 U.S.C. § 2510(15).

[47] 18 U.S.C. § 2702(a)(1).

[48] "Electronic storage" means "(A) any temporary, intermediate storage of a wire or electronic communication incidental to the electronic transmission thereof, and (B) any storage of such communication by an electronic communication service for purposes of backup protection of such communication." 18 U.S.C. § 2510(17).

[49] 18 U.S.C. § 2702(a)(2).

[50] 18 U.S.C. § 2703(a).

[51] Under exigent circumstances, notice of court ordered disclosure may be delayed. 18 U.S.C. § 2705.

[52] 18 U.S.C. § 2703(d). A § 2703(d) order is similar to the Terry rule applied to law enforcement stop and frisks, which requires less than probable cause to believe a crime has been committed, but more than a mere hunch. Terry v. Ohio, 392 U.S. 1, 21 (1968).

[53] 18 U.S.C. § 2703(c).

[54] 18 U.S.C. § 2703(c).

[55] 18 U.S.C. § 2702(a)(1).

[56] Universities that provide e-mail to their students and faculty and companies that provide e-mails to their employees do not constitute "public providers" under the SCA. See Andersen Constulting LLP v. UOP, 991 F. Supp. 1041, 1042- 43 (N.D. Ill. 1998); Orin Kerr, A User's Guide to the Stored Communications Act, and a Legislator's Guide to Amending It, 72 GEO. WASH. L. REV. 1208, 1226 (2004).

[57] 18 U.S.C. § 2702(b).

[58] 18 U.S.C. § 2702(c).

[59] 18 U.S.C. § 2703(a).

[60] 18 U.S.C. § 2703(a), (b). Recall that under exigent circumstances, notice of court ordered disclosure may be delayed. 18 U.S.C. § 2705.

[61] Theofel v. Farey-Jones, 359 F.3d 1066, 1071 (9th Cir. 2003).

[62] Id. at 1075.

[63] 18 U.S.C. § 2510(17).

[64] Theofel, 359 F.3d at 1075.

[65] Id. at 1070.

[66] Id. at 1077.

[67] Illana R. Katana, Cloudy Privacy Protections: Why the Stored Communications Act Fails to Protect the Privacy of Communications in the Cloud, 13 VAND. J. ENT. & TECH. L. 617, 634-35 (2011).

[68] United States v. Weaver, 636 F. Supp. 2d 769, 769-70 (C.D. Ill. 2009).

[69] 18 U.S.C. § 2703(a), (b)(2).

[70] Weaver, 636 F. Supp. 2d at 772.

[71] Id. (citing 18 U.S.C. § 2703(b)(2)).

[72] Crispin v. Christian Audigier, Inc., 717 F. Supp. 2d 965 (C.D. Cal. 2010).

[73] Id. at 969.

[74] Id. at 987.

[75] Id. at 981 (quoting United States v. Steiger, 318 F.3d 1039, 1049 (11th Cir. 2003) ("Thus, the SCA clearly applies, for example, to information stored with a phone company, Internet Service Provider (ISP), or electronic bulletin board system.")).

[76] Citing the Senate Judiciary Committee report issued during congressional consideration of the SCA, the court noted that "to access a communication in such a public system is not a violation of the Act, since the general public has been 'authorized' to do so by the facility provider." Id. at 981 (citing S.Rept. 99-541, at 36 (1986)).

[77] Id. at 981-82.

[78] Id. at 989.

[79] Id. at 991.

[80] Viacom Intern. Inc. v. YouTube Inc., 253 F.R.D. 256 (S.D.N.Y. 2008).

[81] Id. at 264.

[82] 18 U.S.C. § 2702(b)(3).

[83] YouTube Inc., 253 F.R.D. at 265.

[84] Id.

[85] Id.

[86] See supra note 11-14 and accompanying text.

[87] See supra note 20-23 and accompanying text.

[88] United States v. Meriwether, 917 F.2d 955, 960 ("The ECPA does not provide an independent statutory remedy of suppression for interceptions of electronic communications.").

[89] There has been some discussion whether permitting access to the content of e-mails with a subpoena or process less than a probable cause warrant is constitutional under the Fourth Amendment. See Alexander Scolnik, Protections for Electronic Communications: The Stored Communications Act and the Fourth Amendment, 78 FORDHAM L. REV. 349, 393 (2009). The Sixth Circuit, in an as-applied challenge to the SCA in United States v. Warshak held:

The government may not compel a commercial ISP to turn over the contents of a subscriber's e-mails without first obtaining a warrant based on probable cause. Therefore, because they did not obtain a warrant, the government agents violated the Fourth Amendment when they obtained the contents of Warshak's e-mails. Moreover, to the extent that the SCA purports to permit the government to obtain such e-mails warrantlessly, the SCA is unconstitutional.

[90] The Electronic Communications Privacy Act: Government Perspectives on Protecting Privacy in the Digital Age, Hearing Before the Sen. Comm. on the Judiciary 2 (April 6, 2011) (statement of Sen. Patrick J. Leahy) [hereinafter ECPA Hearing].

[91] Id. at 2.

[92] Kerr, supra note 56, at 1243.

[93] ECPA Hearing, supra note 90, at 5 (statement of James Baker, Associate Deputy Attorney General).

[94] There were three bills introduced in the 112th Congress: the Electronic Communications Privacy Act Amendments Act of 2011, S. 1011, 112th Cong., 1st Sess. (2011), filed by Senator Patrick J. Leahy, the ECPA 2.0 Act of 2012, H.R. 6529, 112th Cong., 2d Sess. (2012), filed by Representative Zoe Lofgren, and the Electronic Communications Privacy Act Modernization Act of 2012, H.R. 6399, 112th Cong., 2d Sess. (2012), filed by Representatives Jerrod L. Nadler and John Conyers, Jr. In the 113th Congress, Rep. Lofgren re-introduced her measure, which is now entitled the Online Communication s and Geolocation Protection Act, H.R. 983, 113th Cong., 1st Sess. (2013).

[95] This suppression remedy would be similar to the exclusionary rule under the Fourth Amendment. In the Fourth Amendment context, evidence unlawfully obtained in violation of its prohibition against unreasonable searches and seizures cannot be admitted in a criminal prosecution against the defendant whose rights were violated. Mapp v. Ohio, 367

U.S. 643, 655 (1961). This is known as the exclusionary rule. The Supreme Court has held that the primary purpose of the exclusionary rule is its deterrent effect:

[T]he rule's prime purpose is to deter future unlawful police conduct and thereby effectuate the guarantee of the Fourth Amendment against unreasonable searches and seizures: "The rule is calculated to prevent, not to repair. Its purpose is to deter—to compel respect for the constitutional guaranty in the only effectively available way—by removing the incentive to disregard it.

United States v. Calandra, 414 U.S. 338, 347 (1974) (quoting Linkletter v. Walker, 381 U.S. 618, 637 (1965)).

[96] The legislative history asserts that "[e]xisting telephone companies and electronic mail companies" are examples of electronic communication services. S. Rpt. 99-541, at 14. In Crowley v. CyberSource Corp., the court held that Amazon.com, an on-line retailer, was not an electronic communication service, even though communications could be sent to and from its site. Crowley v. CyberSource Corp., 166 F. Supp. 2d 1263, 1270 (N.D. Cal. 2001).

[97] Kattan, supra note 67, at 654

[98] 18 U.S.C. § 2511(2)(d).

[99] Charles H. Kennedy, An ECPA for the 21st Century: The Present Reform Efforts and Beyond, 20 COMMLAW CONSPECTUS 129, 159 (2011).

[100] 18 U.S.C. § 2721.

[101] Hoffa v. United States, 385 U.S. 293, 301 (1966).

In: The Fourth Amendment
Editor: Lucille E. Huff

ISBN: 978-1-63321-634-1

Chapter 3

DNA DATABANKING: SELECTED FOURTH AMENDMENT ISSUES AND ANALYSIS*

Emily C. Barbour

SUMMARY

Over the past few decades, state and federal lawmakers have promoted the development of databases containing DNA (deoxyribonucleic acid) profiles for individuals who are under the supervision of the criminal justice system due to their known or suspected involvement in a felony or other qualifying crime. Congress has demonstrated concern toward some aspects of DNA databanking by requiring expungement of a DNA profile in certain circumstances, prohibiting most non-forensic uses of DNA profiles and databases, and restricting familial searching. However, in general, Congress has taken a supportive attitude toward DNA databanking and has incentivized the development, expansion, and integration of DNA databases.

As DNA database programs have widened in scope and grown in numbers, their consistency with the Fourth Amendment's prohibition on unreasonable searches and seizures has increasingly been challenged. In the context of compulsory DNA collection, courts have widely upheld laws mandating the collection of DNA from persons who were convicted and are subject to the penal system's custody or supervision. Far fewer cases have addressed whether DNA collection from arrestees is also

* This is an edited, reformatted and augmented version of a Congressional Research Service publication, No. R41847, dated August 16, 2011.

constitutional. The two federal circuit courts of appeals to hear the question upheld the mandatory DNA profiling of *indicted* arrestees, but no federal court has assessed the constitutionality of profiling arrestees in the absence of a judicial finding of probable cause.

Courts have generally upheld the use and permanent storage of a lawfully databanked DNA profile. However, not all courts agree that *any* post-conviction use of those profiles is constitutionally acceptable. In particular, observers are now raising questions about the Fourth Amendment consistency of using databases for non-forensic purposes and for familial searching—that is, using the DNA databases to locate potential relatives of an unidentified suspect. Currently, these concerns are largely confined to the scholarly literature—they have not come before a federal court—and are primarily centered on state database programs. Unlike some state DNA databases, the National DNA Index System (NDIS) and the Combined DNA Index System (CODIS) can not be used for either non-forensic research or intentional familial searching. However, the increase in states that authorize familial searching suggests that it may not be long before the constitutionality of familial searching comes before a federal court.

As these issues percolate up to the courts, new advances and revelations in the science of forensic analysis and databanking may have potentially significant legal implications. Several courts have suggested that new forensic techniques and scientific findings would require them to reevaluate their legal conclusions and analysis. In particular, research into the scope and nature of the information revealed by the "junk" DNA used in forensic analysis may alter how courts measure the intrusiveness of DNA profiling if it suggests that "junk" DNA reveals more sensitive information about its source than scientists previously thought.

INTRODUCTION

In recent years, state and federal laws have facilitated law enforcement's expanded use of deoxyribonucleic acid (DNA) for investigating and prosecuting crimes.[1] These laws authorize compulsory collection of biological matter, which local law enforcement agencies send to the Federal Bureau of Investigation (FBI) for analysis. The FBI then stores unique DNA profiles in a national distributive database, through which law enforcement officials match individuals to crime scene evidence.

Early laws authorized compulsory extraction of DNA only from people convicted for violent or sex-based felonies, such as murder, kidnapping, and offenses "related to sexual abuse"—crimes associated with historically high recidivism rates and for which police were likely to find evidence at crime scenes.[2]

However, in recent decades, new laws have greatly extended the scope of compulsory DNA collection, both by expanding the range of offenses triggering collection authority and, more recently, by authorizing compulsory collection from people who have been arrested but not convicted.

Opponents of DNA databases suggest that DNA databases are "Orwellian" because of the amount of information about private citizens that they put into the control of the government.[3] The most frequent criticism is that the programs violate the Fourth Amendment to the U.S. Constitution.[4] Several federal courts have heard cases alleging that it is unconstitutional for an individual's pre- or post-trial release to be conditioned on DNA collection. Another Fourth Amendment argument, albeit a less litigated one, contends that it is unconstitutional to permit the use of databanked DNA profiles for purposes other than identifying a genetic match with a suspect.

The Fourth Amendment protects individuals' privacy from unreasonable searches and seizures by the government. Federal courts have generally held that compulsory DNA collection from a person who has been convicted of a felony or other qualifying crime and placed under the supervision of the criminal justice system does not constitute an unreasonable search under the Fourth Amendment.[5] These courts found that a convicted felon has a diminished expectation of privacy and that DNA profiling is a minimal intrusion into that privacy.[6] Far fewer cases have given the federal courts an opportunity to decide whether DNA collection from arrestees is also constitutional.

The two federal circuit courts of appeals to hear the question upheld the mandatory DNA profiling of *indicted* arrestees, but no federal court has assessed the constitutionality of profiling arrestees in the absence of a grand jury indictment or judicial finding of probable cause. Similarly, the courts have not yet had an opportunity to articulate the constitutional limits on how databanked DNA profiles may be used.

This report traces the expansion of the statutory authorities for DNA databases and identifies emerging areas of consensus and discord among the federal courts over the Fourth Amendment consistency of compulsory DNA collection and the use of DNA databases. It also predicts additional Fourth Amendment issues that may come before both Congress and the federal courts in the near future.

BACKGROUND ON LAW ENFORCEMENT USE OF DNA

DNA is a complex molecule found in the nucleus and mitochondria of an organism's cells.[7] It consists of two strands of nucleotides, the sequence of which contains the information that forms the basis of the human genetic code. The vast majority of human DNA is exactly the same, but small variations in the sequencing of the nucleotides create people's distinguishing characteristics.[8] Only identical twins share the same DNA profile.[9]

With the help of DNA profiling technology, forensic scientists can examine different regions—or "loci"—of DNA to develop a DNA profile of the person from whom the DNA was extracted.[10] Because forensic analysts examine a select group of loci, the resulting DNA profile may not necessarily be unique to that individual.[11] However, advances in technology have enabled analysts to produce increasingly discriminating profiles. Today, the probability that two unrelated individuals would share a DNA profile derived from an uncontaminated sample of DNA from a cell's nucleus is estimated to be one in a billion at most.[12]

DNA profiles are often compared to fingerprints.[13] As with fingerprints, law enforcement officers collect DNA samples from specific classes of individuals, such as prisoners. However, compulsory DNA collection generally entails blood or saliva samples rather than finger impressions, and DNA profiles can later match any of many types of biological matter obtained from crime scenes.[14] For these reasons, DNA matching is considered a complement to, rather than merely a supplement for, fingerprint analysis in identifying criminal suspects.[15]

The FBI administers DNA storage and analysis for law enforcement agencies across the country. FBI analysts create DNA profiles by "decoding sequences of 'junk DNA.'"[16] So-called "junk DNA" is the name for DNA loci that are "not presently recognized as being responsible for trait coding."[17] Because junk DNA is not currently "associated with any known physical or medical characteristics," its use in forensic analysis prevents, at least for the time being, DNA profiles from containing private or sensitive information about the subject.[18]

Typically, a law enforcement agency's phlebotomist collects a blood or saliva sample from the subject pursuant to state or federal law. The sample may then be analyzed and converted into a DNA profile by a public laboratory (or outsourced by that public lab to a private one) that adheres to the FBI's Quality Assurance Standards.[19] Assuming the laboratory and analyst that generated the profile are adequately credentialed, the resulting DNA profile may then be entered into the Combined DNA Index System (CODIS).[20] CODIS includes DNA profile databases composed at the local, state, and national levels.[21] At the national level, the National DNA Index System (NDIS) facilitates sharing of DNA profiles among participating law enforcement agencies throughout the United States.[22] At each level, profiles are categorized into forensic (crime scene) profiles, offender profiles, and arrestee profiles.[23]

As of March 2011, NDIS contained over 9,535,059 offender profiles.[24] CODIS is primarily evaluated by the number of criminal investigations that CODIS aids.[25] As of March 2011, CODIS had assisted more than 135,500 investigations,[26] suggesting that between 1% and 2% of all samples taken from an offender have assisted a criminal investigation.[27]

STATUTORY FRAMEWORK

The categories of individuals from whom law enforcement officials may require DNA samples have expanded in recent years. The federal government and most states authorize compulsory collection of DNA samples from individuals convicted for specified criminal offenses, including all felonies in most jurisdictions and extending to misdemeanors, such as failure to register as a sex offender or crimes for which a sentence greater than six months applies, in some jurisdictions.[28] In addition, the federal government and some states now authorize compulsory collection from people whom the government has arrested or detained but not convicted. As amended, the DNA Analysis Backlog Elimination Act 2000, discussed below, authorizes compulsory collection from individuals in federal custody, including those detained, arrested, or facing charges, and from individuals on release, parole, or probation in the federal criminal justice system.[29] Under the federal law, if an individual refuses to cooperate, relevant officials "may use or authorize the use of such means as are reasonably necessary to detain, restrain, and collect a DNA sample."[30]

State laws vary, but nearly all states authorize compulsory DNA collection from people convicted for specified crimes, and a small but growing number of states also authorize compulsory collection from arrestees.[31]

Expansion of Statutory Authorities for DNA Profiling

At the federal level, statutory authority for compulsory DNA collection has expanded relatively rapidly. During the 1990s, a trio of federal laws created the logistical framework for DNA collection, storage, and analysis. The DNA Identification Act of 1994 provided funding to law enforcement agencies for DNA collection and created the FBI's Combined DNA Index System to facilitate the sharing of DNA information among law enforcement agencies.[32] Next, the Antiterrorism and Effective Death Penalty Act of 1996 authorized grants to states for developing and upgrading DNA collection procedures,[33] and the Crime Identification Technology Act of 1998 authorized additional funding for DNA analysis programs.[34] The resulting framework centers on CODIS; more than 180 law enforcement agencies throughout the country participate in the system.[35]

In recent years, federal and state laws have expanded law enforcement authority for collecting DNA in at least two ways. First, laws have increased the range of offenses which trigger authority for collecting and analyzing DNA. In the federal context, the DNA Analysis Backlog Elimination Act of 2000 limited compulsory extraction of DNA to people who had been convicted of a "qualifying federal offense."[36] Under the original act, "qualifying federal offenses" included limited but selected felonies, such as murder, kidnapping, and sexual exploitation.[37] After September 11, 2001, the USA PATRIOT Act expanded the "qualifying federal offense" definition to include terrorism-related crimes.[38] In 2004, the Justice for All Act further extended the definition to reach all crimes of violence, all sexual abuse crimes, and all felonies.[39] Similarly, almost all states now authorize collection of DNA from people convicted of any felony.[40]

Second, laws have authorized compulsory DNA collection from people who have been detained or arrested but not convicted on criminal charges. The DNA Fingerprinting Act of 2005 authorized collection "from individuals who are arrested or from non-U.S. persons who are detained under the authority of the United States."[41] The Adam Walsh Child Protection and Safety Act of 2006 subsequently substituted "arrested, facing charges, or convicted" for the word "arrested" in that authority.[42] The U.S. Department of Justice implementing regulations took effect January 9, 2009.[43] Mirroring the statutory language, it requires U.S. agencies to collect DNA samples from "individuals who are arrested, facing charges, or convicted, and from non-United States persons who are detained under authority of the United States."[44] As mentioned, some states have likewise enacted laws authorizing collection of arrestees' DNA.[45] Legislation was proposed in both the 111th and 112th Congress to provide incentives to encourage states to establish processes for collecting DNA from persons arrested for specified state offenses.[46]

As discussed below, courts measure the intrusiveness of DNA databanking programs by considering both the circumstances under which a DNA profile was collected and the uses to which that DNA profile can be put upon its inclusion in a database. It is, therefore, noteworthy that, in addition to expanding the number and variety of circumstances under which DNA profiling is statutorily required, policymakers have expanded the number and variety of purposes for which databanked profiles can be used. In particular, the number of states that permit "familial searching" is increasing. Familial searching is a DNA database search method based on "partial matches" between the DNA profile searched and one—or several—of the DNA profiles in the database.[47] By contrast, a "routine" search of a DNA database compares a complete, well-preserved DNA sample from a single source with the databanked profiles.[48] It is also a "high stringency" search, which means that it is a very discriminating search intended to produce only a "direct match."[49] However, in some circumstances, a crime laboratory seeking to perform a routine search may find it necessary to conduct a lower stringency search, perhaps because the DNA sample being processed is degraded.[50] In that case, the search could generate partial matches that are less accurate than a direct match at predicting the identity of the sample's source.[51]

In some states, partial matches may be recorded and used in a criminal investigation.[52] Although some commentators characterize this method of generating partial matches as a type of familial searching, the FBI does not.[53] According to the FBI, familial searching entails taking a complete and well-preserved DNA sample from a single source and, usually after conducting an unsuccessful high stringency search, conducting a lower stringency search with the intent of generating partial matches.[54] In other words, under the FBI's definition, a familial search is a deliberate database search for potential *relatives* of the suspect—not for the suspect himself.[55] These searches may not be conducted in the National DNA Index System (NDIS),[56] but the FBI has developed provisional procedures for authorizing the release of inadvertently obtained partial match information to law enforcement.[57] As for state databases, some states prohibit familial searching by law[58] or by informal policy,[59] while others have permitted it.[60]

Expungement Provisions

Although Congress has encouraged DNA databanking, it has also constrained the government's authority to use and retain all DNA profiles indefinitely. In particular, federal law mandates expungement of DNA samples upon an arrestee's showing of discharge or acquittal or a convict's showing that the conviction was overturned.[61] These provisions apply to DNA collected by state and local law enforcement officers, in addition to DNA collected in the federal justice or detention systems. However, DNA profiles of convicts who complete their sentences are not eligible for expungement under federal law.

Expungement occurs upon written request; it does not occur automatically.[62] To have a DNA profile expunged from the database, its source must submit, in addition to the written request, a certified copy of a final court order establishing that the conviction was overturned or that charges were dismissed, not filed, or resulted in acquittal.[63]

Fourth Amendment Overview

The Fourth Amendment to the U.S. Constitution provides a right "of the people to be secure in their persons, houses, papers, and effects, against unreasonable searches and seizures."[64] Two fundamental questions arise in every Fourth Amendment challenge. First, does the challenged action constitute a search or seizure by federal or local government and thus trigger the Fourth Amendment right?[65] Second, if so, is the search or seizure "reasonable"?

Search or Seizure

Different tests trigger the Fourth Amendment right depending on whether a litigant challenges government conduct as a seizure or as a search. Seizures involve interference with property rights; a seizure of property occurs when government action "meaningfully interferes" with possessory interests or freedom of movement.[66]

In contrast, searches interfere with personal privacy. Government action constitutes a search when it intrudes upon a person's "reasonable expectation of privacy."[67] A reasonable expectation of privacy requires both that an "individual manifested a subjective expectation of privacy in the searched object" and that "society is willing to recognize that expectation as reasonable."[68]

In general, people have no reasonable expectation of privacy for physical characteristics they "knowingly expos[e] to the public."[69] In evaluating whether people "knowingly expose" identifying characteristics, the Supreme Court has sometimes distinguished the drawing of blood and other internal fluids from the taking of fingerprints. At times, it has signaled that people lack a reasonable expectation of privacy in their fingerprints,[70] but it has held that extraction of blood, urine, and other fluids implicates an intrusion upon a reasonable expectation of privacy, presumably because the former category is "knowingly exposed" to the public while the latter category generally is not.[71]

Under modern Supreme Court precedent, a further complicating factor is that reasonable expectation of privacy depends not only on the type of evidence gathered, but also on the status of the person from whom it is gathered. The inquiry is not simply a yes-or-no determination, but appears to include a continuum of privacy expectations. For example, in *United States v. Knights*,[72] the Court held that the "condition" of probation "significantly diminished" a probationer's reasonable expectation of privacy.[73] This diminished privacy expectation did not completely negate the probationer's Fourth Amendment right; however, it affected the outcome under the Court's Fourth Amendment balancing test.[74]

"Reasonableness" Inquiry When the Fourth Amendment Applies

When government action constitutes a search or seizure, "reasonableness" is the "touchstone" of constitutionality.[75] A search by law enforcement officers is reasonable if supported by a warrant backed by probable cause.[76] However, some searches do not need to meet this warrant standard. For example, searches that entail only a limited intrusion of the suspect's privacy, such as a pat-down, satisfy Fourth Amendment strictures if justified by "reasonable suspicion" based on "specific reasonable inferences."[77] Courts have generally analyzed the Fourth Amendment consistency of DNA databanking programs under yet another reasonableness test: the "general balancing," or "totality-of-the-circumstances" test, which determines the constitutionality of certain "suspicionless" searches that the courts have deemed particularly non-intrusive and/or necessary.[78] This general balancing test weighs the "degree to which [a search or seizure] intrudes upon an individual's privacy" with "the degree to which it is needed for the promotion of legitimate governmental interests."[79]

Historically, courts used the general reasonableness test in three situations: (1) when a routine, administrative purpose justified regular searches; (2) where a long-recognized warrant exception existed, such as for border searches; and (3) where a "special nee[d], beyond the normal need for law enforcement, [made] the warrant and probable cause requirements impracticable."[80] Recently, the Supreme Court cast its Fourth Amendment analysis in "totality-of-the-circumstances" terms in addressing a suspicionless search of a parolee's pockets. In that case, *Samson v. California*,[81] the Court seemed to apply the general balancing test because the petitioner, as a parolee, had diminished legitimate expectations of privacy that were easily outweighed by the state's substantial interests.[82] In other words, the Court found that the search was particularly non-intrusive because the petitioner was subject to the penal system's supervision.

The status of a search's subject within the penal system is now an accepted justification for evaluating the Fourth Amendment consistency of that search under the general reasonableness test.[83] Notably, however, while prisoners, parolees, probationers, and supervised releasees all have diminished privacy rights, their privacy rights are not all diminished equally. Instead, the privacy rights of prisoners, parolees, probationers, and supervised releasees exist on a spectrum.[84] Prisoners have virtually no privacy rights but each subsequent category has slightly greater privacy rights than the one preceding it.

Collecting DNA

The Supreme Court has not accepted a case reviewing a compulsory DNA collection statute. However, the courts have uniformly held that compulsory DNA collection and analysis constitutes a search, and thus triggers Fourth Amendment rights.[85] Accordingly, compulsory DNA collection and profiling laws violate the Fourth Amendment if they fail the reasonableness test.

Prisoners, Parolees, Probationers, and Supervised Releasees

As stated, on the "privacy continuum" prisoners, parolees, probationers, and supervised releasees share diminished, but not necessarily equivalent, privacy rights.[86] Moreover, according to the federal appeals courts, the privacy rights of all four types of convicted offenders are diminished to such an extent that they have no reasonable expectation of privacy in their DNA or DNA profile.[87] Indeed, the vast majority of U.S. Courts of Appeals have upheld either the federal law mandating DNA collection and analysis from prisoners, parolees, and probationers or a similar state law.[88]

In these cases, the only source of conflict between the courts appears to be the appropriate rationale for evaluating these laws under the "totality-of-the-circumstances" test.[89] A majority of courts use the state's court-ordered supervision of the subject as their sole rationale for applying this standard.[90] However, some federal circuit courts of appeals have applied the traditional special needs methodology, assessing whether the collection of the subject's DNA was justified by a "special need beyond the ordinary needs of normal law enforcement" before evaluating whether the government's acquisition and use of the subject's DNA was reasonable under the totality of the circumstances.[91] Although courts have noted this analytical distinction, it may have no practical import because, regardless of the standard applied, courts have consistently upheld compulsory post-conviction DNA collection laws.[92]

Arrestees

To date, only a handful of state[93] and federal[94] judicial decisions address compulsory collection of DNA from persons awaiting a criminal trial, making it difficult to draw conclusions about the constitutionality of this policy. However, recently two federal circuit courts of appeals—the Ninth Circuit and the Third Circuit—held that conditioning an arrestee's pre-trial release on DNA sampling is consistent with the Fourth Amendment. These cases may indicate the approach to this question that other federal circuits are likely to take.

In *United States v. Mitchell*[95] and *United States v. Pool*,[96] the Third and Ninth Circuits respectively upheld the government's request of a criminal arrestee's DNA sample after the arrestee had been indicted but before trial.[97] Both applied the general reasonableness test on the grounds that the subject of the DNA profile was an arrestee and therefore had sufficiently diminished privacy rights to be subjected to reasonable suspicionless searches.[98]

The courts also adopted similar views of the extent to which (1) the arrestee's privacy rights were diminished because of the probable cause determination justifying arrest; (2) DNA collection and databanking intruded upon a person's privacy interests; and (3) DNA profiling served a substantial government interest.

In both cases, the arrestee had been indicted by a grand jury prior to his arrest. For the Ninth Circuit, Pool's indictment was a "watershed event" after which the arrestees' privacy rights were so diminished as to make warrantless and suspicionless searches reasonable.[99] The Third Circuit, however, left undecided whether grand jury indictment — or a judicial finding of probable cause — was a necessary prerequisite for finding that the arrestee had substantially reduced privacy rights.[100] This suggests that, in future cases, courts might find that a person who is detained solely upon the arresting officer's finding of probable cause might have greater privacy rights in his DNA profile than either Mitchell or Pool.[101]

On the extent of the privacy intrusion, both courts characterized DNA profiling as no more intrusive than fingerprinting or photographing a suspect.[102] In adopting this position, the Third Circuit rejected the lower court's description of DNA collection as an act of "information science"—a "quantum leap" in terms of intrusiveness from the "identification science" involved in fingerprinting.[103] Having determined that the only intrusion entailed in DNA collection was the identification of the arrestee, the Third Circuit wrote that the indictment and subsequent arrest of a person deprives the arrestee of any legitimate privacy right in anonymity.[104]

The Third and Ninth Circuits also agreed that the government's interests in DNA databanking are sufficiently important to outweigh any privacy intrusion created by DNA collection. In *Pool*, the Ninth Circuit stated that the government had two "substantial" interests in DNA profiling: (1) identifying the arrestee so as to determine who is in government custody and whether that person may have been involved in other crimes; and (2) discouraging the arrestee from violating the conditions of pre-trial release.[105] The Third Circuit in *Mitchell* characterized the "most compelling" government interest as the accurate identification of arrestees, reasoning that this information helps the state determine whether or not the arrestee should be detained pending trial.[106] Moreover, the Third Circuit wrote, the government needs this information "as soon as possible," which means that the government's interest in identifying the arrestee is not served equally well by collecting his DNA *after* conviction rather than before it.[107]

USING AND RETAINING DATABANKED DNA

In addition to the constitutionality of compulsory DNA collection, a second set of emerging Fourth Amendment issues with DNA database programs concerns the retention and use of DNA samples and profiles. For example, in *United States v. Mitchell*,[108] discussed above,[109] the arrestee argued that the indefinite retention of his DNA profile would violate the Fourth Amendment.[110] However, the Third Circuit declined to reach the merits of his argument because Mitchell's DNA sample had not yet been collected, rendering its potential retention not yet ripe for judicial review.[111]

Federal law requires the FBI to expunge DNA profiles for people who receive acquittals or whose convictions are overturned.[112] Courts have pointed to these provisions as reducing the intrusiveness of collecting DNA samples from arrestees.[113] This case law suggests that sources of lawfully collected and databanked DNA maintain some degree of privacy interests in their DNA profiles. However, it is not clear whether *convicted* felons retain those rights as well, and, if they do, what types of actions would unreasonably intrude upon those rights.

Post-Sentence Privacy Rights

The federal expungement provisions do not address storage of DNA from people who have successfully completed their sentences. Rather, once a person's DNA profile has been entered into CODIS database, "police at any level of government with a general criminal investigative interest ... can tap into that DNA without any consent, suspicion, or warrant, long after his period of supervised release ends."[114] Convicted felons who have completed their sentences have initiated Fourth Amendment challenges to the government's indefinite storage of their DNA profiles and samples.[115] However, few courts have been convinced by their arguments. In particular, judicial skepticism of genetic exceptionalism has made it difficult for defendants to overcome the established constitutionality of the government's indefinite retention of fingerprints and other identification records of convicted felons.[116]

Nevertheless, like the cases over DNA collection from an arrestee, cases upholding the government's use and storage of databanked DNA after its source completes his sentence diverge. In particular, dicta in state and federal court opinions augur judicial divergence over the extent to which an offender retains privacy rights in his DNA sample and profile after his full release from the penal system.

The First Circuit acknowledged this apparent dissensus in its 2010 case, *Boroian v. Mueller*.[117] In that case, the court upheld the government's indefinite retention and periodic matching of a felon's DNA after his sentence was completed.[118] However, it also expressly refused to hold "as some courts have suggested" that, upon a DNA sample's lawful extraction and databanking, its source "loses a reasonable expectation of privacy with respect to *any* subsequent use of that profile."[119] Instead, the First Circuit ruled that, once a qualified offender's DNA "profile has been lawfully created and entered into CODIS ... the FBI's retention and periodic matching of the profile against other profiles in CODIS for the purpose of *identification* is not an intrusion on the offender's legitimate expectation of privacy."[120] In other words, *Boroian* suggests that there could be circumstances in which the post-sentence retention and use of a DNA profile violate its source's reasonable expectation of privacy.

As the First Circuit in *Boroian* pointed out, however, several state courts have not reached such a limiting conclusion,[121] and their more expansive view may have support within the federal judiciary. For example, the Supreme Court of the State of Hawaii held in *State v. Hauge*[122] that "once a blood sample and DNA profile is lawfully procured from a defendant, *no* privacy interest ... in either the sample or the profile" prevents its indefinite use and retention by the government.[123] Significantly, Judge Easterbrook of the U.S. Court of Appeals for the Seventh Circuit expressed support for this perspective in his concurrence in the 2004 case *Green v. Berge*,[124] in which he wrote that lawfully obtained DNA samples may be put to a wide variety of uses beyond indefinite storage and periodic matching because "the Fourth Amendment does not control how properly collected information is deployed."[125]

Informational Privacy Rights

The difference between the First Circuit's view in *Boroian* and Judge Easterbrook's opinion in *Green* has significant implications for the potential uses of DNA databases and the information they contain. Database opponents characterize laws that authorize or condone the use of DNA databases to research anything other than a suspect's identity as making the database program particularly intrusive.[126] Although these concerns have yet to form the basis of a Fourth Amendment challenge to a DNA databanking program, they are premised on a belief that people retain a substantial privacy interest in the information encoded in their DNA even after they have been convicted and their DNA lawfully included in a DNA database.

Academic Research and Non-forensic Information

Congress has generally sought to restrict the non-forensic use of DNA databases to those with the potential to enhance the forensic utility of CODIS.[127] The DNA Analysis Backlog Elimination Act of 2000 criminalized both (1) the knowing disclosure of a sample or DNA analysis to someone who is not authorized to receive it and (2) the unauthorized acquisition or use of such a sample or analysis.[128] However, federal law does not also entitle individuals aggrieved by the misuse of their profiles to pursue a private cause of action against those responsible.[129] In other words, federal law prohibits most non-forensic uses of DNA databases but does not specifically authorize private individuals to enforce this prohibition.

While database opponents would like to see federal law incorporate a private cause of action, their primary concern is with state laws that permit a wider range of non-forensic uses of state DNA databases. Some state legislatures, for example, have expressly authorized the use of the state DNA database for medical and academic research.[130] In the eyes of database opponents, these states have established databanking programs that are more intrusive for the purposes of the Fourth Amendment than those that follow the stricter federal standards.[131]

Although these claims have not been raised before a federal judge, they can draw support from language in existing case law. Several courts have considered, as part of their Fourth Amendment analysis, both the range of purposes for which a given DNA database can be used and the penalties for any misuse.[132] However, courts have also indicated that, until a case presents facts establishing that a DNA database was used for a non-forensic purpose, a court cannot accurately measure any resulting privacy intrusion or assess its Fourth Amendment reasonableness.[133]

Familial Searching and Information About Genetic Relationships

Although concerns about possible non-forensic use of DNA databases are reflected in state and federal laws, the universe of possible *forensic* uses of DNA databases has generated greater public concern in recent years. In particular, the technique known as "familial searching" has received widespread media attention—both positive and negative—over the last decade.[134]

The FBI defines a familial search as a deliberate database search for potential *relatives* of the suspect. Federal courts have not yet had an occasion to assess the constitutionality of familial searching. The arrestee in *United States v. Mitchell*,[135] discussed above,[136] argued that one reason that developing his DNA profile is more intrusive than obtaining his fingerprints is that, through the former, the government can obtain information about his biological relationships and any criminal activity by a member of his family.[137] However, the court did not address this argument in its analysis, finding, *inter alia*, that Mitchell had failed to provide any evidence to establish the possibility that his DNA—which had not yet been collected—would be used in this way.[138]

Some privacy interests implicated by familial searching are different from those implicated by more routine DNA database searches.[139] In particular, commentators have asserted that familial searching may violate two types of—and more than one person's—privacy interests.[140] The first type is the privacy interests of the person whose DNA profile was located as a partial match. Commentators assert that this person has a privacy interest in information about his genetic relationships, information that may be revealed by a familial search of the DNA database.[141] The second set of privacy interests belongs to family members of the person whose profile was a partial match.[142] Law enforcement may violate these privacy rights if, while following up on the lead provided by the partial match, they collect DNA from the partial match's family members without a warrant.[143] These family members may have privacy interests in their genetic identities as well as in their genetic relationship—or lack thereof—with the person whose DNA was profiled.

Because the constitutionality of familial searching has not yet reached the federal courts, the existence of a reasonable privacy interest in genetic relationships remain a largely untested assertion. Commentators defend its existence on the grounds that, unlike other types of information, people do not knowingly expose their genetic relationships and, moreover, may not necessarily be credited with knowledge—let alone amenability to public exposure—of their genetic kin.[144]

IMPLICATIONS OF NEW RESEARCH ON JUNK DNA

Despite the "rapid pace of technological development in the area of DNA analysis,"[145] much of DNA's scientific value remains a mystery. As mentioned, FBI analysts rely on junk DNA precisely because it is not believed to reveal sensitive medical or biological information. Partly for that reason, proponents of expansive DNA collection argue that any privacy intrusion resulting from DNA storage or analysis is minimal at most. For example, when he introduced the amendment that authorizes collection and analysis of DNA from arrestees in the federal system, Senator Kyl emphasized that storage of DNA samples would not intrude upon individuals' privacy rights, stating that "the sample of DNA that is kept ... is what is called 'junk DNA'—it is impossible to determine anything medically sensitive from this DNA."[146] Likewise, courts have assumed that DNA analysis and storage involves only a minimal privacy intrusion.

However, language in some opinions suggests that this assumption might change if scientists discover new uses for junk DNA. The First, Second, and Third Circuits have all suggested that "discovery of new uses for 'junk DNA' would require a reevaluation of the [Fourth Amendment] reasonableness balance."[147]

In addition, at least two judges on the Ninth Circuit have expressed concern about the potential for profiles developed from junk DNA to yield more sensitive information about their sources in the future.[148]

Scientific research on junk DNA is still emerging, and some research suggests that junk DNA contains more genetic information than previously assumed. For example, in October 2008, University of Iowa researchers released study findings showing that junk DNA has the potential to "evolve into exons, which are the building blocks for protein-coding genes."[149] Other scientists have similarly hypothesized that there are "gems among the junk" in DNA.[150]

Hence, a remaining question is whether use of junk DNA will continue to offer superficial identifying information or whether it will reveal more detailed medical or biological characteristics.

CONCLUSION

The nation, all 50 states, and many localities have adopted some type of DNA database program. Over time, Congress and state legislatures have expanded the types of crimes and circumstances that can result in DNA collection and databanking. Congress has demonstrated concern toward some aspects of DNA databanking by requiring expungement of a DNA profile in certain circumstances, prohibiting most non-forensic uses of DNA profiles and databases, and restricting familial searching.

However, in general, Congress has taken a supportive attitude toward DNA databanking and incentivized the development, expansion, and integration of DNA databases.

As DNA database programs have widened in scope and grown in numbers, their consistency with the Fourth Amendment's prohibition on unreasonable searches and seizures has increasingly been challenged. In the context of compulsory DNA collection, courts have widely upheld laws mandating the collection of DNA from persons who were convicted and are subject to the penal system's custody or supervision. Far fewer cases have given the federal courts an opportunity to decide whether DNA collection from arrestees is also constitutional. The two federal circuit courts of appeals to hear the question upheld the mandatory DNA profiling of *indicted* arrestees, but no federal court has assessed the constitutionality of profiling arrestees in the absence of a judicial finding of probable cause.

Courts have generally upheld the indefinite use and storage of a lawfully databanked DNA profile after its source's conviction. However, not all courts agree that *any* post-conviction use of those profiles is constitutionally acceptable. In particular, observers are now raising questions about the Fourth Amendment consistency of using databases for non-forensic purposes and for familial searching. Currently, these concerns are largely confined to the scholarly literature—they have not come before a federal court—and primarily centered on state database programs. Unlike some state DNA databases, the National DNA Index System (NDIS) and the Combined DNA Index System (CODIS) can not be used for either non-forensic research or intentional familial searching. However, the increase in states that authorize familial searching suggests that it may not be long before the constitutionality of familial searching comes before a federal court.

Much of the Fourth Amendment analysis of these issues depends on the current state of scientific knowledge on DNA and, more importantly, "junk" DNA—that is, the subset of DNA used to create databanked profiles. Decisions upholding DNA databanking programs have often described junk DNA as empty or meaningless genetic material because it is believed to reveal no sensitive information about its source. However, recent scientific research is challenging the accuracy of this description. While it may be too early for courts to give weight to this new research as fact, some have suggested that the constitutionality of DNA database programs should be reevaluated if "junk" DNA is ultimately found to reveal sensitive genetic information.

End Notes

[1] For more on the progression of federal legislation authorizing use of DNA, see CRS Report R41800, *DNA Testing in Criminal Justice: Background, Current Law, Grants, and Issues*, by Nathan James.

[2] For example, offenses triggering DNA collection authority under the original DNA Analysis Backlog Elimination Act of 2000, P.L. 106-546 (2000), included murder, voluntary manslaughter, and other offense relating to homicide; offenses relating to sexual abuse, sexual exploitation or other abuse of children, or transportation for illegal sexual activity; offenses relating to peonage and slavery; kidnapping; offenses involving robbery or burglary; certain offenses committed within Indian territory; and attempt or conspiracy to commit any of the above offenses.

[3] Banks v. United States, 490 F.3d 1178, 1180 (describing the arguments of DNA database critics as allusions "to a police state reminiscent of George Orwell's dystopia portrayed in *1984*"). *See, e.g.*, United States v. Sczubelek, 402 F.3d 175, 194 n.11 (3rd Cir. 2005) (McKee, J., dissenting) (characterizing the DNA Act as ushering in an "Orwellian intrusion"); United States v. Kincade, 379 F.3d 813, 870 (9th Cir. 2004) (Reinhardt, J., dissenting) ("The compulsory extraction of blood samples and the maintenance of permanent DNA profiles of American citizens is, unfortunately, the beginning not the end. 1984 arrives twenty years later than predicted.").

[4] Litigants have also brought challenges under the Eighth and Fourteenth Amendments to the U.S. Constitution as well as under other legal and constitutional theories. *See* Hon. Donald E. Shelton, *Twenty-First Century Forensic Science Challenges for Trial Judges in Criminal Cases: Where the Polybutadiene Meets the Bitumen*, 18 WIDENER L. J. 309, 361-62 (2009) (listing different theories used to challenge the constitutionality of DNA database and compulsory collection statutes). *See also* United States v. Pool, 645 F. Supp.2d 903 (9th Cir. 2009) (rejecting challenges under Fourth, Fifth, and Eighth Amendments to the U.S. Constitution). However, this report is limited to a discussion of challenges brought under the Fourth Amendment.

[5] *E.g.*, United States v. Weikert, 504 F.3d 1 (1st Cir. 2007); United States v. Amerson, 483 F.3d 73 (2d Cir. 2007), *cert. denied* 552 U.S. 1042 (2007); Wilson v. Collins, 517 F.3d 421 (6th Cir. 2006); United States v. Hook, 471 F.3d 766 (7th Cir. 2006), *cert. denied* 549 U.S. 1343 (2007); United States v. Kraklio, 451 F.3d 922 (8th Cir. 2006), *cert. denied* 549 U.S. 1044 (2006); United States v. Kriesel, 508 F.3d 941 (9th Cir. 2007); United States v. Banks, 490 F.3d 1178 (10th Cir. 2007); United States v. Castillo-Lagos, 147 Fed. App'x. 71 (11th Cir. 2005).

[6] *See, e.g.*, *Weikert*, 504 F.3d at 27, 30-33 (finding that a convicted felon on supervised release "has a substantially diminished expectation of privacy" and collecting a blood sample is a "minimal" intrusion that is not meaningfully augmented by the government's subsequent use of that sample to create and databank a DNA profile); *Amerson*, 483 F.3d at 29 (finding that the appellants have "diminished" expectations of privacy and the collection of their DNA for a DNA database is a "small" intrusion of privacy).

[7] For a more in-depth discussion of DNA and its use in law enforcement, see CRS Report R41800, *DNA Testing in Criminal Justice: Background, Current Law, Grants, and Issues*, by Nathan James.

[8] *See* Human Genome Program, U.S. Department of Energy, *Primer on Molecular Genetics* (Washington, DC, 1992), http://www.ornl.gov/hgmis/publicat/primer/primer.pdf.

[9] United States v. Kincade, 379 F.3d 813, 818 n.7 (9th Cir. 2004) (en banc), *cert. denied*, 544 U.S. 924 (2005).

[10] In the United States, forensic scientists use "short tandem repeat" technology to analyze 13 DNA loci. Department of Energy, *Human Genome Project Information: DNA Forensics*, at http://www.ornl.gov/sci/techresources/ Human_Genome/elsi/forensics.shtml.

[11] NATIONAL POLICING IMPROVEMENT AGENCY, NATIONAL DNA DATABASE ANNUAL REPORT 2007-2009, 7 (2009).

[12] *See id.*; NATIONAL INSTITUTE OF JUSTICE, USING DNA TO SOLVE COLD CASES, 5-7 (2009), *available at* http://www.ncjrs.gov/pdffiles1/nij/194197.pdf.

[13] The term "DNA fingerprinting" was coined in 1985. L.A. Foreman et. al., *Interpreting DNA Evidence: A Review*, 71 INT'L STATISTICAL REVIEW 473, 474 (2003) (giving credit to a 1985 article in *Nature* for coining the term). However, the analogy between fingerprinting and DNA profiling has since drawn criticism from both the legal and scientific communities. *See, e.g.*, Foreman, *supra*, at 474 (describing the term "DNA fingerprinting" as "misleading"); United States v. Mitchell, 681 F. Supp.2d 597, 608 (W.D. Pa. 2009) (criticizing the comparison as "pure folly"). Given this criticism, a frequently used argument against DNA databases is "genetic exceptionalism"—that is, the theory that DNA profiles are fundamentally different from other types of identification and medical records. George J. Annas, *Genetic Privacy*, in DNA AND THE CRIMINAL JUSTICE SYSTEM: THE TECHNOLOGY OF JUSTICE 135, at 136-37 (David Lazer ed., 2004).

[14] Under federal statute and analogous state laws, officials collect DNA from "tissue, fluid, or other bodily sample." *See* 42 U.S.C. §14135a(c)(1). To facilitate especially "reliable" DNA analysis, FBI guidelines direct federal law enforcement officials to rely on blood samples. *See Kincade*, 379 F.3d at 817.

[15] DNA-Sample Collection and Biological Evidence Preservation in the Federal Jurisdiction, 73 Fed. Reg. at 74933-34.

[16] *Amerson*, 483 F.3d at 76.

[17] *Kincade*, 379 F.3d at 818.

[18] *See id.* at 818, 837 (suggesting that, by virtue of looking only at the subject's junk DNA, the government's invasion of the subject's privacy is minimal); H.R. Rep. No. 106-900 at 27.

[19] JOHN M. BUTLER, FUNDAMENTALS OF FORENSIC DNA TYPING 270 (2010). In addition to signing a memorandum of understanding agreeing to adhere to these standards, state laboratories submitting DNA profiles to the National DNA Index System must also be accredited and audited annually. *Id.* at 271.

[20] DNA INITIATIVE, COMBINED DNA INDEXING SYSTEM, http://www.dna.gov/dna-databases/codis.

[21] DNA INITIATIVE, LEVELS OF THE DATABASE, http://www.dna.gov/dna-databases/levels.

[22] *See* FEDERAL BUREAU OF INVESTIGATION, COMBINED DNA INDEX SYSTEM (CODIS), http://www.fbi.gov/about-us/lab/ codis/codis.

[23] DNA Initiative, Levels of the Database, *supra* note 21.

[24] FEDERAL BUREAU OF INVESTIGATION, CODIS—NDIS STATISTICS, http://www.fbi.gov/about-us/lab/codis/ndisstatistics.

[25] *Id.*

[26] *Id.*

[27] *See id. See also* Michael T. Risher, *Warrantless Collection of DNA From People Merely Accused of a Crime Raises Not Only Privacy Concerns But Also Questions About Efficacy*, 88 CRIM. L. REP. 320 (December 15, 2010) (stating that, according to FBI statistics, the

"hit" rate as of September 2010 was 1.4%). The FBI also breaks down the number of offender profiles and investigations aided by state on its website. Federal Bureau of Investigation, CODIS—NDIS Statistics, *supra* note 24. For a more detailed synthesis and overview of studies regarding the utility of DNA databases to criminal investigations, see CRS Report R41800, *DNA Testing in Criminal Justice: Background, Current Law, Grants, and Issues*, by Nathan James.

[28] For more information on state laws regarding compulsory DNA collection, see NATIONAL CONFERENCE OF STATE LEGISLATURES, CRIMINAL JUSTICE DNA DATABASE (2010), http://www.ncsl.org/default.aspx?tabid=21808..

[29] 42 U.S.C. §14135a. *See also* 18 U.S.C. §3142(b) ("The judicial officer shall order the pretrial release of the person [charged with an offense] ... subject to [*inter alia*] the condition that the person cooperate in the collection of a DNA sample from the person if the collection of such a sample is authorized pursuant to section 3 of the DNA Analysis Backlog Elimination Act of 2000 ...").

[30] 42 U.S.C. §14135a(a)(4)(A).

[31] *See* NATIONAL CONFERENCE OF STATE LEGISLATURES, CRIMINAL JUSTICE DNA DATABASE (2010), http://www.ncsl.org/default.aspx?tabid=21808 (indicating 24 states that authorize DNA collection from arrestees). However, many of the state laws authorizing collection from arrestees limit the scope of such collection to people arrested for specified violent or serious crimes.

[32] P.L. 103-322, 108 Stat. 2065 (1994) (codified at 42 U.S.C. §§14131-14134).

[33] P.L. 104-132, 110 Stat. 1214 (1996).

[34] P.L. 105-251, 112 Stat. 1871 (1998).

[35] *See* FEDERAL BUREAU OF INVESTIGATION, CODIS BROCHURE, http://www.fbi.gov/about-us/lab/codis/codis_brochure.

[36] 42 U.S.C. §14135a(a)(1)(B).

[37] P.L. 106-546, §3, 114 Stat. 2726, 2729-30 (2000).

[38] P.L. 107-56, §503, 115 Stat. 272, 364 (2001).

[39] P.L. 108-405, §203(b), 118 Stat. 2260, 2270 (2004) (codified at 42 U.S.C. §14135a(a)(2)).

[40] *See* NATIONAL CONFERENCE OF STATE LEGISLATURES, CRIMINAL JUSTICE DNA DATABASE (2010), http://www.ncsl.org/default.aspx?tabid=21808.

[41] DNA Fingerprint Act of 2005, Tit. X, P.L. 109-162, 119 Stat. 2960. 42 U.S.C. §14135a(a)(1).

[42] Adam Walsh Child Protection and Safety Act of 2006, sec. 155, P.L. 109-248, 120 Stat. 587 (2006) (codified at 42 U.S.C. §14135a(a)(1)).

[43] DNA-Sample Collection and Biological Evidence Preservation in the Federal Jurisdiction, 73 Fed. Reg. at 74,932, 74,935.

[44] 28 C.F.R. §28.12(b).

[45] *See, e.g.*, Kan. Stat. Ann. §21-2511(e)(2) (authorizing DNA collection from individuals arrested for any felony or certain other crimes); N.M. Stat. §29-16-6(B) (authorizing collection of DNA samples from individuals arrested for specific violent felonies); Va. Code Ann. §19.2-310.2:1 (requiring collection of DNA samples from "arrested for the commission or attempted commission of a violent felony").

[46] Katie Sepich Enhanced DNA Collection Act of 2011, H.R. 988, 112th Cong. (2011); Katie Sepich Enhanced DNA Collection Act of 2011, S. 517, 112th Cong. (2011); Katie Sepich Enhanced DNA Collection Act of 2010, H.R. 4614, 111th Cong. (as passed the House, May 18, 2010). Specifically, the legislation would authorize incentive grants and bonus payments for states that institute a "minimum" or "enhanced" "DNA collection process," respectively. A "minimum" process entails searching the federal DNA database "at least one time"

against samples from individuals "arrested for or charged with" specified types of state offenses, such as those including an element of sexual contact that are punishable by at least five years imprisonment. An "enhanced" process requires the collection of samples, to be included in the federal database, from individuals "arrested for or charged with" a broader range of state law offenses, such as those with a sexual conduct element that are punishable by more than one year imprisonment. For an overview of existing federal grant programs related to the collection and law enforcement use of DNA, see CRS Report R41800, *DNA Testing in Criminal Justice: Background, Current Law, Grants, and Issues*, by Nathan James.

[47] *See* FEDERAL BUREAU OF INVESTIGATION, FREQUENTLY ASKED QUESTIONS (FAQS) ON THE CODIS PROGRAM AND THE NATIONAL DNA INDEX SYSTEM, http://www.fbi.gov/about-us/lab/codis/codis-and-ndis-fact-sheet.

[48] *See id.*; Jessica D. Gabel, *Probable Cause from Probable Bonds: A Genetic Tattle Tale Based on Familial DNA*, 21 HASTINGS WOMEN'S L. J. 3, 17-18 (2010).

[49] *See* FBI, *supra* note 47; Gabel, *supra* note 48, at 17.

[50] *See* FBI, *supra* note 47; Gabel, *supra* note 48, at 17.

[51] *See* FBI, *supra* note 47; Gabel, *supra* note 48, at 17.

[52] For a map of states that permit partial matching and familial searching and those that do not, see COUNCIL FOR RESPONSIBLE GENETICS, STATE RULES ON PARTIAL/FAMILIAL SEARCHING, http://www.councilforresponsiblegenetics.org /dnadata/usa/usa2.html.

[53] *See* FBI, *supra* note 47; Gabel, *supra* note 48, at 17. *See also* Natalie Ram, *DNA Confidential*, SCIENCE PROGRESS (November 2, 2009), *available at* http://www.scienceprogress.org /2009/11/dna-confidential (referring to this method as "partial match reporting" rather than "familial searching").

[54] FBI, *supra* note 47. *See* Gabel, *supra* note 48, at 18.

[55] *See* Gabel, *supra* note 48, at 18.

[56] FBI, *supra* note 47. *See* Gabel, *supra* note 48, at 18.

[57] FBI, *supra* note 47; U.S. Department of Justice, *Federal Bureau of Investigation Interim Plan for the Release of Information In the Event of a "Partial Match" at NDIS*, (July 20, 2006), http://www.bioforensics.com/conference08/ Familial_Searches/CODIS_Bulletin.pdf.

[58] *See, e.g.*, MD. CODE ANN., Public Safety, §2-506(d) (prohibiting searches of the state DNA database "for the purpose of identification of an offender in connection with a crime for which the offender may be a biological relative of the individual from whom the DNA sample was acquired").

[59] According to the Council for Responsible Genetics, several states, including Alaska, Maine, Michigan, and Vermont, include prohibitions on either partial match or familial searching in lab manuals. Council for Responsible Genetics, *supra* note 52. *See also* Ram, *supra* note 53 (stating that research revealed that at least 12 states have unwritten policies on partial match reporting or familial searching).

[60] *See, e.g.*, Press Release, Governor McDonnell Announces Virginia Department of Forensic Science to Begin Using Familial DNA Searches in Virginia (March 21, 2011), *available at* http://www.governor viewRelease.cfm?id=648 (announcing that the Virginia Department of Forensic Science developed the capability to perform familial searches and issued a policy for considering requests from law enforcement officials to conduct these searches).

[61] 42 U.S.C. §14132(d).

[62] *See* FEDERAL BUREAU OF INVESTIGATION, CODIS—EXPUNGEMENT POLICY, http://www.fbi.gov/about-us/lab/codis/codis_expungement. *See also* Sonia M. Suter, *All in*

the Family: Privacy and DNA Familial Searching, 26 HARV. J. L. & TECH. 309, 341 (2010) (stating that exonerated arrestees and offenders may not be informed about the possibility of having their DNA records expunged and, even if they are, the procedures for getting the profile expunged may be overly burdensome).

[63] 42 U.S.C. §14132(d). *See also* FBI, *supra* note 62 (detailing procedures for expungement).

[64] U.S. CONST. amend. IV.

[65] Courts have applied the Fourth Amendment to state and local government actions since 1961, when, in *Mapp v. Ohio*, the Supreme Court interpreted the Fourteenth Amendment as having incorporated the Fourth Amendment to the states. 367 U.S. 643, 655 (1961).

[66] *See* United States v. Place, 462 U.S. 696, 716 (1983) (Brennan, J., concurring in result); Michigan v. Summers, 452 U.S. 692, 696 (1981).

[67] Some justices and experts have noted the circularity of the combination of this definition and the general Fourth Amendment "reasonableness" inquiry. *See, e.g.*, Minnesota v. Carter, 525 U.S. 83, 97 (1998) (Scalia, J., concurring). However, such criticisms have not yet caused the Court to reconsider its test, except perhaps for the narrow category of interiors of homes, for which the Court has found a near-automatic reasonable expectation of privacy by virtue of privacy in the home having "roots deep in the common law." *See* Kyllo v. United States, 533 U.S. 27, 34 (2001).

[68] *Kyllo*, 533 U.S. at 33 (citing California v. Ciraolo, 476 U.S. 207, 211 (1986)).

[69] Katz v. United States, 389 U.S. 347, 351 (1967).

[70] *See, e.g.*, Davis v. Mississippi, 394 U.S. 721, 727 (1969) ("Fingerprinting involves none of the probing into an individual's private life and thoughts that marks an interrogation or search."). Later, in *Hayes v. Florida*, the Supreme Court seemed to suggest that fingerprinting does constitute a search, 470 U.S. 811, 814 (1985) (referring to fingerprinting as less intrusive than *other* types of searches and seizures), a shift in keeping with the Court's broader trend toward classifying more activity as constituting a search and leaving the heart of the constitutional analysis for the Fourth Amendment "reasonableness" inquiry. Thus, it appears that although the Court views the drawing of blood as a greater intrusion than fingerprinting, both activities now qualify as searches.

[71] *See, e.g.*, Skinner v. Ry. Labor Executives' Ass'n, 489 U.S. 602, 616 (1989) ("We have long recognized that a 'compelled intrusio[n] into the body for blood to be analyzed for alcohol content' must be deemed a Fourth Amendment search" (quoting Schmerber v. California, 384 U.S. 757, 767-768 (1966)).

[72] 534 U.S. 112 (2001).

[73] *Id.* at 119-120.

[74] *Id.*

[75] *Id.* at 118.

[76] *See* Atwater v. City of Lago Vista, 532 U.S. 318, 354 (2001).

[77] Alabama v. White, 496 U.S. 325, 330 (1990); Terry v. Ohio, 392 U.S. 1, 21-22, 27 (1968).

[78] *See, e.g.*, United States v. Pool, 621 F.3d 1213, 1218-19 (9th Cir. 2010); Wilson v. Collins, 517 F.3d 421, 426 (6th Cir. 2008).

[79] Samson v. California, 547 U.S. 843, 848 (2006).

[80] Griffin v. Wisconsin, 483 U.S. 868, 873 (1986) (citing New Jersey v. T.L.O., 469 U.S. 325, 351 (1985) (Blackmun, J., concurring)).

[81] 547 U.S. 843 (2006).

[82] *Id.* at 847, 847 n.1.

[83] *See id. See also* United States v. Knights, 534 U.S. 112, 114-120 (2001) (evaluating a warrantless search of a probationer's home under the general reasonableness test because

the conditions placed on his probation significantly diminished the reasonableness of his expectation of privacy); Griffin v. Wisconsin, 483 U.S. 868, 873-74 (1986) (applying the general reasonableness test to a search of a person's home because the person was on probation).

[84] *See, e.g.*, Wilson v. Collins, 517 F.3d 421, 425 n.2, 426-27 (6th Cir. 2008) (describing a "privacy continuum" on which "a parolee ... has less diminished privacy rights than a prisoner"). Parole and supervised release are sometimes conflated, but they represent two distinct forms of post-incarceration supervision by the state. *See* UNITED STATES SENTENCING COMMISSION, 2010 FEDERAL SENTENCING GUIDELINES MANUAL 484 (2010), *available at* http://www.ussc.gov/Guidelines/2010_guidelines. Whereas parolees are on release from incarceration *before* the end of their sentence, supervised releasees are serving a term of state supervision *after* their initial term of incarceration. *See id.*

[85] *See, e.g.*, United States v. Amerson, 483 F.3d 73, 77 (2d Cir. 2007), *cert. denied* 552 U.S. 1042 (2007) ("It is settled law that DNA indexing statutes, because they authorize both a physical intrusion to obtain a tissue sample and a chemical analysis to obtain private physiological information about a person, are subject to the strictures of the Fourth Amendment.").

[86] *See Wilson*, 517 F.3d at 425 n.2.

[87] *See, e.g.*, United States v. Weikert, 504 F.3d 1, 3 (1st Cir. 2007) (upholding provision of the federal law mandating DNA collection from a supervised releasee); United States v. Amerson, 483 F.3d 73, 89 (2d Cir. 2007) (upholding provisions of the federal law mandating DNA collection from a probationer); *Wilson*, 517 F.3d at 423 (upholding a state law mandating DNA collection from a prisoner).

[88] *E.g., Weikert*, 504 F.3d at 3 (holding for the First Circuit that the federal law is consistent with the U.S. Constitution); *Amerson*, 483 F.3d at 89 (upholding the federal law), *cert. denied* 552 U.S. 1042 (2007); United States v. Hook, 471 F.3d 766 (7th Cir. 2006) (upholding the federal law), *cert. denied* 549 U.S. 1343 (2007); United States v. Kraklio, 451 F.3d 922 (8th Cir. 2006) (upholding the federal law), *cert. denied* 549 U.S. 1044 (2006); United States v. Kriesel, 508 F.3d 941, 942 (9th Cir. 2007) (upholding the federal law); United States v. Banks, 490 F.3d 1178 (10th Cir. 2007) (upholding the federal law); United States v. Castillo-Lagos, 147 Fed. App'x. 71 (11th Cir. 2005) (upholding the federal law); Jones v. Murray, 962 F.2d 302 (4th Cir. 1992) (upholding the Virginia statute). *See also* Padgett v. Donald, 401 F.3d 1273 (11th Cir. 2005) (upholding the Georgia statute); Green v. Berge, 354 F.3d 675 (7th Cir. 2004) (upholding the Wisconsin statute); Shaffer v. Saffle, 148 F.3d 1180 (10th Cir. 1998) (upholding the Oklahoma statute); Schlicher v. Peters, 103 F.3d 940 (10th Cir. 1996) (upholding the Kansas statute); Boling v. Romer, 101 F.3d 1336 (10th Cir. 1996) (upholding the Colorado statute).

[89] *See Amerson*, 483 F.3d at 78 (stating that the courts have nearly unanimously upheld state and federal DNA databanking laws, but, in doing so, have used two different approaches); *Kraklio*, 451 F.3d at 924 ("The only disagreement among the circuits is what analytical approach to use in upholding the [DNA collection] statutes."); United States v. Kincade, 379 F.3d 813, 830-31 (9th Cir. 2004) ("Confronted with challenges to the federal DNA Act and its state law analogues, our sister circuits and peers in the states have divided in their analytical approaches" between a traditional special needs analysis and a direct assessment of reasonableness).

[90] *See, e.g., Wilson*, 517 F.3d at 426 (finding that the direct application of the general balancing test is appropriate in a case involving a prisoner). *See also Amerson*, 483 F.3d at 78

(describing the Second Circuit's insistence on the traditional special needs test methodology as in conflict with the Third, Fourth, Fifth, Ninth, and Eleventh Circuits).

[91] *See, e.g., Amerson*, 483 F.3d at 78-80 (articulating the traditional methodology of a special needs test, justifying its application to compulsory DNA collection laws, and applying it).

[92] *See, e.g., Wilson*, 517 F.3d at 427 n. 4 ("Even if we were to apply the more stringent special-needs test, there is no reason to believe the ultimate result would be different.").

[93] This report focuses on federal court decisions, but several state courts have also reviewed the collection of DNA from arrestees, with mixed results. For example, the Virginia Supreme Court upheld Virginia's statute authorizing DNA collection from arrestees. Anderson v. Virginia, 650 S.E.2d 702 (Vir. 2006), *cert. denied*, 553 U.S. 1054 (2008). In contrast, the Minnesota Court of Appeals held that a state law authorizing collection of a DNA sample "upon a finding of probable cause, but before any conviction ..." violated the Fourth Amendment to the U.S. Constitution and Article 1, Section 10 of the Minnesota Constitution. In the Matter of the Welfare of C.T.L., 722 N.W.2d 484, 486 (Minn. Ct. App. 2006).

[94] In addition to the two federal district court cases discussed in this report, two other federal judicial decisions, both issued in December 2009, are of interest. First, in *Friedman v. Boucher*, the U.S. Court of Appeals for the Ninth Circuit denied Nevada police officers' motion for qualified immunity where the officers, acting on their own volition rather than pursuant to any state or federal law, forced the collection of DNA from a man in pre-trial detention for the purpose of comparing his DNA to evidence available in "cold cases." 580 F.3d 847 (9th Cir. 2009). The Ninth Circuit emphasized the lack of statutory authority and the absence of a strong governmental interest in the case. Given those fact-specific underpinnings for its decision, it is unclear whether the Ninth Circuit's rationale would apply in a future case in which statutory authority and a different governmental interest existed. Second, in *Haskell v. Brown*, the U.S. District Court for the Northern District of California denied a motion to enjoin the enforcement of a California statute requiring the collection of DNA from adults arrested for felony offenses. 677 F. Supp. 2d 1187 (N.D.Cal. 2009). Because the case arose at the preliminary injunction stage, it is unclear how much weight the decision might have on a future challenge to California's law.

[95] United States v. Mitchell, No. 09-4718, 2011 U.S. App. LEXIS 15272 (3d Cir. July 25, 2011), *rev'g* 681 F.Supp.2d 597 (W.D.Pa. 2009).

[96] United States v. Pool, 621 F.3d 1213 (9th Cir. 2010), *aff'g* 645 F. Supp.2d 903 (E.D. Cal. 2009).

[97] In *Pool*, the defendant was granted pre-trial release. For that reason, a provision of the Bail Reform Act, 18 U.S.C. §3142(b), which requires DNA collection as a condition of pre-trial release, provided a supplementary basis of statutory authority.

[98] *See Mitchell*, 2011 U.S. App. LEXIS at *43; *Pool*, 621 F.3d at 1218-19 (writing that the judicial or grand jury finding of probable cause for an arrest was a "watershed event" after which arrestees' privacy rights were so diminished as to make certain suspicionless searches reasonable).

[99] *Pool*, 621 F.3d at 1218-19.

[100] *Mitchell*, 2011 U.S. App. LEXIS at *71, n.22 ("[W]e need not reach the question of whether any additional probable cause requirement other than the requirements inherent in the statute—that an individual is arrested—is necessary.").

[101] *See id.*

[102] *Id.* at 2011 U.S. App. LEXIS at *64-65; *Pool*, 621 F.3d at 1221-22.

[103] *Mitchell*, 681 F.Supp.2d at 609.

[104] *See id.*
[105] *Pool*, 621 F.3d at 1223.
[106] *Id.* at 76, 79.
[107] *Id.* at 79-80.
[108] United States v. Mitchell, No. 09-4718, 2011 U.S. App. LEXIS 15272 (3d Cir. July 25, 2011).
[109] *Supra* notes 95-107 and accompanying text.
[110] *Mitchell*, 2011 U.S. App. LEXIS at *71-72.
[111] *Id.* at 72.
[112] 42 U.S.C. §14132(d).
[113] *See, e.g., Pool*, 621 F.3d at 1227 n.16 ("The alleged intrusion on any of Pool's rights is also reduced by the provision that the DNA sample may be expunged if he is not found guilty or his case is dismissed.").
[114] United States v. Kriesel, 508 F.3d 941, 952 (9th Cir. 2007).
[115] *See, e.g.*, Boroian v. Mueller, 616 F.3d 60, 68 n.6 (1st Cir. 2010); United States v. Amerson, 483 F.3d 73 (2d Cir. 2007); Johnson v. Quander, 440 F.3d 489, 499 (D.C. Cir. 2006).
[116] *See, e.g., Boroian*, 616 F.3d at 67 ("[I]dentification records of convicted felons, such as fingerprints or mugshots, are routinely retained by the government after their sentences are complete and may be expunged only in narrowly defined circumstances ... [P]recedents hold that the government's matching of a lawfully obtained identification record against other records in its lawful possession does not infringe on an individual's legitimate expectation of privacy."); United States v. Amerson, 483 F.3d 73, 86 (2d Cir. 2007) ("[I]t is well established that the state need not destroy records of identification—such as fingerprints, photographs, etc.—of convicted felons, once their sentences are up. The same applies to DNA."); Johnson v. Quander, 440 F.3d 489, 499 (D.C. Cir. 2006) ("Police departments across the country could face an intolerable burden if every 'search' of an ordinary fingerprint database were subject to Fourth Amendment challenges. The same applies to DNA fingerprints ... CODIS operates much like an old-fashioned fingerprint database (albeit more efficiently)."). *See also* Stevenson v. United States, 380 F.2d 590 (D.C. Cir.), *cert. denied*, 389 U.S. 962 (1967) (holding that a defendant had no constitutional right to the expungement of his mugshots and fingerprints after his conviction was set aside).
[117] 616 F.3d 60 (1st Cir. 2010).
[118] *Id.* at 68.
[119] *Id.* (emphasis in original).
[120] *Id.*
[121] *Id. See also* State v. Hauge, 79 P.3d 131, 144 (Haw. 2003) (holding that the defendant had no reasonable privacy interest in his DNA sample or profile after it had been lawfully collected); Patterson v. State, 742 N.E.2d 4, 16-17 (Ind. Ct. App. 2000) ("[S]ociety is not prepared to recognize as reasonable [the defendant's] continued expectation of privacy in blood samples *lawfully* collected by police" (emphasis in original)).
[122] 79 P.3d 131 (Haw. 2003)
[123] *Id.* at 144 (Haw. 2003) (emphasis added).
[124] 354 F.3d 675 (7th Cir. 2004) (Easterbook, J., concurring).
[125] *Id.* at 680.
[126] *See, e.g.*, Sonia M. Suter, *supra* note 62, at 335 (contending that familial searching could unlawfully invade the privacy of the "offender or arrestee, his family members, and the family itself" and expressing concern over the possibility that, in some states, a DNA database could be used to conduct research on its sources' traits and diseases); Gabel, *supra*

note 48, at 4-5 (arguing that cases involving familial DNA searches "raise legitimate concerns about the rise of the silent informant" and "represent a troubling addition to the increasing collection, retention, and use of genetic information"). *See also* Memorandum from Seth Axelrad for The American Society of Law, Medicine and Ethics (ASLME), *available at* http://www.aslme.org/dna_04/reports/axelrad3.pdf (describing different state policies toward the non-forensic use of DNA databases).

[127] *See* 42 U.S.C. §14132(b)(3) (authorizing the use of DNA profiles in CODIS for forensic identification purposes, related legal proceedings, and, once personally identifiable information is removed, a "population statistics database"). *See also* D.H. Kaye, *Behavioral Genetics and Criminal DNA Databases*, 69 LAW & CONTEMP. PROBS. 259, 276 (2006) (explaining how population statistics databases, protocol development, and quality control research all fit within the "identification paradigm").

[128] P.L. 106-546, §3(a)(5), *codified at* 42 U.S.C. §14135e(c).

[129] *Compare e.g., id.* (making the knowing or intentional disclosure or use of a confidential DNA forensic record or analysis a felony but not establishing a private cause of action for the aggrieved individual) *with* RI GEN. LAWS §12- 1.5-15 (criminalizing violations of the confidentiality conditions on the use of DNA samples and authorizing a person aggrieved by a violation to bring a civil action for damages, injunctive relief, and attorneys' fees) *and* VT. STAT. ANN. tit. 20, §1941 (criminalizing violations of the confidentiality conditions on the use of DNA samples and authorizing a person aggrieved by a violation to pursue a private action for all "appropriate relief").

[130] *See, e.g.*, MICH. COMP. LAWS §28.176(2)(d) (permitting DNA profiles contained in the database to be used, *inter alia*, for an "academic," "research," or "statistical" analysis if "personal identifications" are removed); Ala. Code §36- 18-31 (authorizing the creation of a "DNA population statistical database" that may be used to, *inter alia*, "provide data relative to ... disease or disability" and "assist in other humanitarian endeavors including, but not limited to, educational research or medical research or development"). *See also* ARK. CODE ANN. §12-12-1018(d) (authorizing the creation of a "population database" composed of DNA samples stored in the database with the "personal identification" removed).

[131] *See, e.g.*, Suter, *supra* note 62, at 335, 338 (stating that "vague legislative limits on the uses of the samples" risk, if not empower, government searches that exceed their legal boundaries and raise "civil liberty concerns by increasing the extent and breadth of government intrusions"). *But see* Kaye, *supra* note 127, at 260 (rejecting some of the theories, both legal and scientific, that underpin this argument). Database opponents are also concerned that not all states have expressly prohibited using DNA databases—and the information contained therein—for non-forensic research. *See, e.g.*, Suter, *supra* note 62, at 336 (stating that there are 40 jurisdictions that neither authorize nor prohibit non-forensic uses and, in those states, there is "uncertainty as to the legal limits" on the uses of stored samples). For example, Idaho lists permissible uses of collected DNA samples and profiles but does not expressly prohibit potential non-forensic uses. IDAHO CODE ANN. §§19-5505, 19-5514.

[132] *See, e.g.*, Banks v. United States, 490 F.3d 1178, 1192, 1193 (10th Cir. 2007) (weighing "the plaintiffs' diminished privacy rights, the minimal intrusion involved in obtaining a DNA sample, *and the Act's restrictive provisions*" against the governmental interests (emphasis added)); United States v. Amerson, 483 F.3d 73, 85 (2d Cir. 2007) (finding that the privacy invasion occasioned by the maintenance of DNA profiles is minimal because, *inter alia*, "the Act severely limits the circumstances and purposes for which the DNA profiles can be released").

[133] *See Amerson*, 483 F.3d at 87; United States v. Kincade, 379 F.3d 813, 837-38 (9th Cir. 2004).

[134] *See, e.g.*, Maura Dolan, *State to Double Crime Searches Using Family DNA*, L.A. TIMES (May 9, 2011); Jessica Cerretani, *Whodunit?* BOSTON GLOBE (October 31, 2010); Natasha Singer, *In Fighting Crime, How Far Should a Genetic Net Reach?* N.Y. TIMES (July 24, 2010); Jeffrey Rosen, *Genetic Surveillance for All*, SLATE (March 17, 2009), http://www.slate.com/id/2213958.

[135] United States v. Mitchell, No. 09-4718, 2011 U.S. App. LEXIS 15272 (3d Cir. July 25, 2011).

[136] *Supra* notes 95-107 and accompanying text.

[137] *Mitchell*, 2011 U.S. App. LEXIS at * 62-64, n.19.

[138] *Id.*

[139] *See, e.g.*, Suter, *supra* note 62, at 327-28.

[140] *See, e.g., id.* at 342.

[141] *See, e.g., id.* at 342, 343.

[142] *See Mitchell*, 2011 U.S. App. LEXIS at * 63, n.19 (suggesting that the subject of a DNA profile lacks standing to assert the Fourth Amendment rights of his biological relatives in keeping their genetic kinship with him private).

[143] *See, e.g.*, State v. Athan, 158 P.3d 27, 33-34 (Wash. 2007) (upholding the constitutionality of collecting DNA by posing a fictitious law firm, inviting the suspect to join a class action lawsuit via mail, and collecting his saliva from the sealed return envelope). *See also* Suter, *supra* note 62, at 358 (suggesting that a partial match alone cannot satisfy the probable cause test because current forensic testing does not establish a sufficiently high probability of a biological connection between the source of the partial match and the suspect).

[144] *See, e.g.*, Suter, *supra* note 62, at 364 (listing circumstances in which the source of the databanked profile with similarities to the suspect's may be unaware that he had a sibling who was given up for adoption or that one of his children is the product of his partner's adultery).

[145] United States v. Weikert, 504 F.3d 1, 3 (1st Cir. 2007).

[146] 151 CONG. REC. S13757 (daily ed. December 16, 2005) (statement of Sen. Kyl).

[147] United States v. Mitchell, No. 09-4718, 2011 U.S. App. LEXIS 15272, at *60 (3d Cir. July 25, 2011) ("Should technological advancements change the value of 'junk DNA,' reconsideration of our Fourth Amendment analysis may be appropriate."); United States v. Stewart, 532 F.3d 32, 36 (1st Cir. 2008); United States v. Amerson, 483 F.3d 73, 85 n.13 (2d Cir. 2007) ("Should the uses to which 'junk DNA' can be put be shown in the future to be significantly greater than the record before us today suggests, a reconsideration of the reasonableness balance would be necessary"). *See also* Haskell v. Brown, 677 F. Supp. 2d 1187, 1190 n.1 (N.D. Cal. 2009) (noting that "so-called 'junk' DNA might someday be found to contain genetic programming material," but stating that the court's opinion must be based on "the facts as they are ... today.").

[148] For example, in *Pool*, Judge Lucero wrote separately from the Ninth Circuit's majority opinion to emphasize that, if, in the future, a litigant proved that a CODIS DNA profile yields information unavailable from a fingerprint or photograph, the "defendant's interests could be vastly different" from Pool's and the "totality-of-the-circumstances test" would need to be conducted anew. *Pool*, 621 F.3d at 1230-31 (Lucero, concurring). In *Kincade*, Judge Reinhardt wrote in his dissenting opinion that "The fact that scientists currently lack the capacity to comprehend the full significance of the data stored within junk DNA samples *is irrelevant*" to the Fourth Amendment analysis because the DNA profiles are retained forever and the advance of science will make them "only more revealing in time." 345 F.3d at 850 (emphasis added).

[149] Lin L, Shen S, Tye A, Cai JJ, Jiang P, et al., *Diverse Splicing Patterns of Exonized Alu Elements in Human Tissues*, 4 PLOS GENETICS 1 (2008), http://www.plosgenetics.org /article/info%3Adoi%2F10.1371%2Fjournal.pgen.1000225.

[150] W. Wayt Gibbs, *The Unseen Genome: Gems Among the Junk*, 29 SCI. AM. 49 (2003), http://www.imb.uq.edu.au/ download/large/TheUnseenGenome.pdf.

In: The Fourth Amendment
Editor: Lucille E. Huff
ISBN: 978-1-63321-634-1

Chapter 4

LAW ENFORCEMENT USE OF GLOBAL POSITIONING (GPS) DEVICES TO MONITOR MOTOR VEHICLES: FOURTH AMENDMENT CONSIDERATIONS*

Alison M. Smith

SUMMARY

As technology continues to advance, what was once thought novel, even a luxury, quickly becomes commonplace, even a necessity. Global Positioning System (GPS) technology is one such example. Generally, GPS is a satellite-based technology that discloses the location of a given object. This technology is used in automobiles and cell phones to provide individual drivers with directional assistance. Just as individuals are finding increasing applications for GPS technology, state and federal governments are as well. State and federal law enforcement use various forms of GPS technology to obtain evidence in criminal investigations. For example, federal prosecutors have used information from cellular phone service providers that allows real-time tracking of the locations of customers' cellular phones. Title III of the Omnibus Crime Control and Safe Streets Act of 1958 (P.L. 90-351) regulates

* This is an edited, reformatted and augmented version of the Congressional Research Service Publication, CRS Report for Congress R41663, dated November 22, 2011.

the interception of wire, oral, and electronic communications. As such, it does not regulate the use of GPS technology affixed to vehicles and is beyond the scope of this report. However, bills introduced in the 112th Congress, such as S. 1212 and H.R. 2168, would address circumstances under which law enforcement may obtain, use, or disclose GPS data.

The increased reliance on GPS technology raises important societal and legal considerations. Some contend that law enforcement's use of such technology to track motor vehicles' movements provides for a safer society. Conversely, others have voiced concerns that GPS technology could be used to reveal information inherently private. Defendants on both the state and federal levels are raising Fourth Amendment constitutional challenges, asking the courts to require law enforcement to first obtain a warrant before using GPS technology.

Subject to a few exceptions, the Fourth Amendment of the U.S. Constitution requires law enforcement to obtain a warrant before conducting a search or making a seizure. Courts continue to grapple with the specific issue of whether law enforcement's use of GPS technology constitutes a search or seizure, as well as the broader question of how the Constitution should address advancing technology in general. The Supreme Court may provide some answers in *United States v. Jones* (131 S.Ct. 3064 (2011)) when it addresses the issue of whether law enforcement's use of GPS technology in connection with motor vehicles falls within the Fourth Amendment's purview. Lower federal courts have arrived at varying conclusions. Several district and circuit courts of appeals have concluded that law enforcement's current use of GPS technology does not constitute a search, and is thus permissible, under the Constitution. One circuit court has found the duration of GPS tracking to be constitutionally significant. State legislatures and state courts have approached the issue in various ways. Some states have enacted laws requiring law enforcement to obtain a warrant before using GPS technology. Some state courts have resolved the question under their own constitutions. Other state courts have relied on Supreme Court precedent, such as *United States v. Knotts*, 460 U.S. 276 (1983), to derive an answer.

This report discusses the basics of GPS technology, society's reliance on it, and some of the related legal and privacy implications. In addition, the report examines legislative and judicial responses on both federal and state levels.

GLOBAL POSITIONING SYSTEM (GPS) TECHNOLOGY

GPS "is a satellite-based technology that reveals information about the location, speed, and direction of a targeted subject. While it was initially developed for the U.S. military, countless civilian applications of GPS appear in the marketplace."[1] For example, many people rely on an automotive GPS device when they travel[2] for navigational directions, or even to find dining options. Similarly, some companies equip their vehicles with built-in GPS devices that allow a command center to know a vehicle's location upon its involvement in an accident or track it if it is stolen.[3] Pet collars have been outfitted with GPS devices to enable owners to locate their lost pets.[4] Campers and hikers use portable GPS devices to determine their location and map out their journey.[5] Cellular phones are embedded with GPS devices to synchronize time changes when a person leaves a certain time zone.[6] Cartographers use GPS devices to make maps and surveyors to determine property boundaries.[7] Airlines use them to pilot and locate planes.[8] In short, not only are Americans finding an increased interest in GPS technology, but it is becoming an essential aspect of many Americans' day-to-day lives.[9]

Law Enforcement's Uses of GPS Technology

The military and private sector are not alone in their interests and reliance on GPS technology. Federal and state governments have also incorporated it into many of their domestic activities. Examples include tracking stranded motorists and predicting natural disasters such as earthquakes, tsunamis, hurricanes, etc. Such tracking allows for more effective emergency preparedness and relief to victims.[10]

Increasingly, law enforcement relies on and finds new uses for GPS technology to assist in monitoring and gathering evidence.[11] For example, sex offenders are outfitted with ankle monitors to track their movements 24 hours a day. Also, consider the following examples, taken by various state law enforcement authorities:

- After 11 attacks on women were reported during a six-month period in two Virginia counties, police installed a GPS device on the van owned by a man who lived near the crime scenes. The suspect was a convicted rapist who had served 17 years in prison. By tracking his movements with the device, police were able to intercept him in Falls

Church, VA, where he was dragging a woman to a remote area. The series of assaults ceased after his arrest.[12]

- Wisconsin police, acting on a tip about a former methamphetamine manufacturer, attached a GPS device to the suspect's car without first obtaining a warrant. Information recorded on the device led them to a large tract of land visited by the suspect. With the consent of the landowner, they searched the property and found paraphernalia used to manufacture methamphetamines. The suspect was subsequently arrested.[13]
- Police in New York used evidence acquired from a GPS device (attached without first obtaining a warrant) that had been attached to a burglary suspect's car a year earlier. The device, which monitored the suspect's movement without interruption for more than two months, showed that the suspect had driven by a burglarized store. This evidence was used to corroborate a witness's testimony that the suspect had been observing the store to determine its vulnerable points.[14]
- In California, the Los Angeles Police Department "outfit[ted] its cruisers with air guns that can launch GPS-enabled 'darts' at passing cars."[15] Once affixed to a vehicle, police can track it in real time from police headquarters. The air guns are generally used in situations requiring immediate action such as a high-speedchase.[16]

Most new cellular phones include GPS capabilities.[17] As a result, federal prosecutors have been known to get information from cellular phone service providers that allows real time tracking of the locations of customers' cellular phones.[18] In one case, information obtained from a cellular phone's GPS helped prove that a key suspect had been within a mile of a murder scene. In another case, a Mexican drug-cartel truck was tracked. The truck was carrying over two tons of cocaine.[19]

While there are many substantial benefits to the use of GPS technology, some have voiced concerns. Many of these concerns arise from law enforcement's use of GPS technology without first obtaining a warrant to either attach the device or monitor the suspect after the device has been attached. Some have argued that the warrantless use of GPS technology has the potential of interfering with individual privacy, protected by the Fourth Amendment to the United States Constitution.[20] Legal scholars assert that a warrant ensures that the police have probable cause to believe that criminal activity is taking place or is imminent, thus preventing unwarranted intrusion into a person's freedom and private life.[21] Others contend that GPS tracking is analogous to law enforcement conducting public surveillance with its own eyes or with surveillance cameras or radio transmitting beepers. Therefore, some courts and legal scholars believe a warrant is unnecessary and the Fourth Amendment does not apply.[22]

THE FOURTH AMENDMENT

The Fourth Amendment to the United States Constitution, which protects "[t]he right of the people to be secure ... against unreasonable searches and seizures,"[23] governs and circumscribes searches and seizures[24] made by the federal and the state governments.[25] The Amendment's operative text can be divided into two clauses. The first clause forbids the government from conducting any search or seizure that is "unreasonable." The second clause prohibits the government from issuing a warrant unless it is obtained based "upon probable cause," is "supported by Oath," and contains particularized descriptions of the "place to be searched" and what is "to be seized." Although "[t]here is nothing in the amendment's text to suggest that a warrant is required to make a search or seizure reasonable,"[26] the U.S. Supreme Court has long since read these two clauses together, generally holding that a warrantless search or seizure is presumptively (if not per se) unreasonable.[27] The Fourth Amendment does not apply, however, unless the government's conduct constitutes a search or seizure within the meaning of the Amendment, that is, where there is a justifiable expectation of privacy. In addition, even when the Amendment does apply, "because the ultimate touchstone of the Fourth Amendment is 'reasonableness,' the warrant requirement is subject to certain exceptions."[28]

At one time, the purpose of the Fourth Amendment was seen as a protection of people's property rights against unlawful physical trespasses.[29] However, it gradually came to be seen as a protection of something more.[30] "[T]he principal object of the Fourth Amendment," the Court has explained, "is the protection of privacy rather than property."[31] In addition, "the Fourth Amendment protects people—and not simply 'areas'—against unreasonable searches and seizures."[32] Thus, in its seminal decision in *Katz v. United States*,[33] the Court held that police officers violated the Fourth Amendment when they conducted a warrantless search using a listening and recording device placed on the outside of a public phone booth to eavesdrop on the conversation of a suspect who had "'justifiably relied' upon ... [the privacy of the] telephone booth."[34] The Court concluded that the Fourth Amendment protects both a person and that person's expectation of privacy from warrantless searches or seizures in places which are justifiably believed to be private.

It is not enough, however, for a person to have a subjective "expectation of privacy," for any person might claim that she expected privacy at any time and in any place. Indeed, many might argue that the police conduct a search by simply watching them. Therefore, they will reason, because the police did not have a warrant, they violated the Constitution and the evidence obtained cannot be used against them.[35] However, the Court has rejected such broad interpretations of the term "search," holding instead "that visual observation is no 'search' at all."[36] Simply put, "the police cannot reasonably be expected to avert their eyes from ... activity that could have been observed by any member of the public. Hence, '[w]hat a person knowingly exposes to the public, even in his own home or office, is not a subject of Fourth Amendment protection.'"[37]

In applying the principles set forth in *Katz* to determine whether law enforcement has conducted a search or a seizure within the meaning of the Fourth Amendment, the Court frequently cites *Katz*'s concurring opinion. The concurring opinion clarified the Court's test as being "whether a person has a 'constitutionally protected reasonable expectation of privacy.'"[38] Courts presently examine law enforcement's conduct to make this threshold determination by following "a two-part inquiry: first, has the individual manifested a subjective expectation of privacy in the object of the challenged search? Second, is society willing to recognize that expectation as reasonable?"[39]

The Fourth Amendment and Technology

State and federal courts have long since wrestled with whether and how to apply the *Katz* test to advancing technology. For example, the Supreme Court in *Katz* determined that when the suspect entered the phone booth and shut the door, he had a reasonable expectation of privacy that his telephone conversation would be private. Thus, the police conducted an unreasonable search by using a listening and recording device without getting a warrant. Similarly, in *Kyllo v. United States*,[40] the Court decided that a suspect had a reasonable expectation of privacy in his home when the police, suspecting him of growing marijuana, used a thermal imaging device without a warrant to detect the heat emanating from it. In contrast, when the Court was asked in *United States v. Ciraolo*[41] to decide whether a suspect had a reasonable expectation of privacy in a back yard he surrounded with a 10-foot-high fence, the Court concluded that police observation from an airplane in public air space was not a search; thus, no warrant was necessary.

Likewise, the Court found that a defendant did not have a reasonable expectation of privacy in his car while traveling along public roads. In *United States v. Knotts,*[42] Minnesota law enforcement officers placed (with the seller's consent) a beeper in a chloroform container, believing that the defendant buyer was engaging in the production of illicit drugs. Officers subsequently followed the vehicle carrying the container, maintaining both a visual surveillance and a monitor receiving the beeper signals. Based on the beeper signals, the officers tracked the container to the defendant's secluded cabin. After a three-day visual surveillance of the cabin, the officers obtained and executed a search warrant and found the container and a drug laboratory in the cabin. The defendant sought to have the evidence suppressed, arguing that the warrantless monitoring of the beeper violated the Fourth Amendment.

The Court disagreed and held that the officers' actions did not constitute a search or seizure, as the defendant did not have a legitimate expectation of privacy. The beeper signal was not used to monitor movement of the container within a private residence. Instead, it was used to monitor movement along public highways and other areas visible to the naked eye.

However, in a similar scenario, when a beeper was activated while inside various suspects' homes, the Court held that suspects with interests in those respective homes did have a reasonable expectation of privacy and that the absence of a warrant constituted an unreasonable search.[43] In *United States v. Karo,*[44] Drug Enforcement Administration (DEA) agents installed an electronic beeper in a can of ether with the consent of the owner (a government informant). The marked can was sold with others to the defendants, who intended to use the contents for cocaine production. Having tracked the can to several residences and storage facilities, law enforcement determined the can's location and obtained an arrest warrant. The defendants were arrested and charged with possession of cocaine with intent to distribute. One of the defendants sought to have the evidence suppressed as "tainted fruit" of an unlawful search. This case presented two issues for the Court to address: (1) whether the beeper's installation constituted a search or seizure when the container was delivered to a buyer without any knowledge of the beeper's presence and (2) whether the beeper's monitoring within an individual's residence falls within the Fourth Amendment's ambit when it reveals information that could not have been obtained through visual surveillance.

As to the first issue, the Court found that the defendant lacked a Fourth Amendment interest, as the then-owner's consent was sufficient to withstand the challenge. [45] However, the Court found that the Fourth Amendment was violated when the agents used the beeper to locate the container in a private dwelling without first obtaining a search warrant. Although the transfer of the beeper to the defendant did not violate the Fourth Amendment, the monitoring of the beeper in a private residence not open to visual surveillance did violate the Fourth Amendment.[46]

GPS MONITORING: STATES' RESPONSES

States have employed various approaches toward the use of GPS technology. Some states have addressed the issue statutorily by enacting laws "imposing civil and criminal penalties for the [improper] use of electronic tracking devices or expressly requiring exclusion of evidence produced by such a device unless obtained by the police acting pursuant to a warrant."[47] Judicially, state courts have reached differing conclusions. State courts in New York, Washington, Oregon, Delaware, and Massachusetts have determined that, absent some exigent circumstance, police officers must first obtain a warrant before using GPS technology (in some cases the court is interpreting its respective state constitution).[48] For example, in *State v. Weaver*,[49] the Court of Appeals of New York held that the "unconsented placement" of a GPS tracking device and subsequent monitoring of the vehicle constituted a search requiring a warrant under the state's constitution.[50] The court noted that it has interpreted its constitution to provide greater protections than the Fourth Amendment "in the areas of search and seizure."[51] The court found that the defendant had a reasonable expectation of privacy that was infringed by the state's action. While the court found that the defendant had a diminished expectation of privacy, "that expectation was not reduced to zero."

Conversely, state courts in Nevada and Virginia have found that GPS use does not raise any state or federal constitutional concerns.[52] In *Foltz v. Commonwealth*,[53] the Virginia court found that the law enforcement's use of a GPS tracking device to track a vehicle's movement on a public street did not constitute a search or seizure under either the federal or state constitutions. The defendant, a registered sex offender on probation for committing sexual assault, became a suspect in a new series of sexual assaults. Police attached a

GPS device to the defendant's work vehicle. Observing "in real time via a computer screen with a map,"[54] police noticed that the van was driven in and out of various neighborhoods where crimes had occurred. After another sexual assault occurred, the police followed the defendant the next day and witnessed him grab a woman and knock her down to the ground. The police stopped the assault and arrested the defendant. In reaching its decision, the court concluded that the defendant did not manifest a subjective expectation of privacy while driving down the street looking for victims. Moreover, the court concluded that the defendant "did nothing to prevent others from inspecting the bumper of the work van." Many states have not addressed the issue of GPS tracking either legislatively or judicially as of this writing.

GPS Monitoring: Federal Courts

The Supreme Court has not directly addressed the issue of whether law enforcement's use of GPS technology in connection with motor vehicles falls within the Fourth Amendment's purview. Lower federal courts have relied on Supreme Court precedent on other types of monitoring to arrive at arguably varying conclusions on GPS tracking.

Several district and circuit courts of appeals have concluded that law enforcement's current use of GPS technology does not constitute a search and is thus permissible under the Constitution.[55] For example, in *United States v. Pineda-Moreno*,[56] the 9th Circuit decided a case involving a criminal drug investigation in Oregon. Without a warrant, DEA agents attached a GPS device to a Jeep owned by a man suspected of drug activity. The device was attached on several occasions over a four-month period.[57] Four times agents attached the device while the Jeep was parked on a public street; one time while it was parked at a public parking lot; and two times while it was parked on his property, necessitating that agents sneak onto it in the early morning hours.[58] Eventually, the GPS "device alerted agents that [the suspect's] vehicle was leaving a suspected marijuana grow site." The suspect was then arrested and officers found marijuana in the Jeep.[59]

The court held that the DEA's actions did not constitute a search because a person does not have a reasonable expectation of privacy in a car's exterior, even when the car is parked on the person's driveway (unless the person has affirmatively sought to exclude others from entering his land).[60] The court then held that the DEA's monitoring of the suspect's travel was analogous to the facts in *Knotts*, where the police followed the suspect's car by using a beeper on the theory that using the GPS device disclosed information that the police "could have obtained by following the car."[61] The court then concluded by quoting *Knotts*: "'Insofar as [Pineda-Moreno's] complaint appears to be simply that scientific devices such as the [tracking devices] enabled the police to be more effective in detecting crime, it simply has no constitutional foundation. We have never equated police efficiency with unconstitutionality and decline to do so now.'"[62]

Similar to *Pineda-Moreno*, many of the courts to follow this line of reasoning also have analogized GPS devices to the beeper devices in *Knotts*. In addition, many have also included a reservation similar to the one the Supreme Court made in *Knotts*. In *Knotts*, the defendant argued that the Court's ruling would permit the government to conduct warrantless and unlimited surveillance with such technology: "[I]f such dragnet type law enforcement practices as the defendant envisions should eventually occur," the Court responded, "there will be time enough then to determine whether different constitutional principles may be applicable."[63] It is unclear what this "dragnet reservation" means, and the differing outcomes in the federal circuits can be attributed to how the courts interpret it. The 9th Circuit, quoting with approval the 7th Circuit, stated it this way: "Should [the] government someday decide to institute programs of mass surveillance of vehicular movements, it will be time enough to decide whether the Fourth Amendment should be interpreted to treat such surveillance as a search."[64]

Conversely, the D.C. Circuit held that law enforcement's prolonged use of GPS technology to track a particular vehicle does amount to a search and thus requires a warrant.[65] In *United States v. Maynard*,[66] the court found that *Knotts*'s "dragnet warning" applied to an individual when the law enforcement's warrantless surveillance was constant and protracted, and that the reservation was not limited to mass surveillance of multiple vehicles. In this case, the Federal Bureau of Investigation (FBI) installed a GPS device on a vehicle to track the "movements" of a club owner suspected of conspiracy to distribute cocaine. They monitored him "[for] 24 hours a day for 28 days as he moved among scores of places, thereby discovering the totality and pattern of his movements from place to place to place."[67] The information was subsequently used as evidence at trial to prove his involvement in the conspiracy.[68]

The court distinguished its holding from the decisions in the other circuits by noting that the rule in *Knotts* was limited. Whereas the other circuits had read *Knotts*'s dragnet reservation to mean "mass surveillance," the court read it to apply as well to individual, prolonged "'twenty-four hour surveillance.'"[69]

The court also concluded that a person has a reasonable expectation of privacy in the totality of his movements over the course of a month, which he does not actually or constructively expose to the public, even though law enforcement could constitutionally conduct warrantless observation of his individual movements from one place to another while in public.[70] The Supreme Court granted certiorari review in this case[71] raising questions as to whether and when the warrantless use of a GPS tracking device on a motor vehicle might violate the Fourth Amendment.

DIFFERING DECISIONS

Reading the decisions to date, it is unclear whether there is a split in Fourth Amendment jurisprudence over use of GPS technology as such, or the cases reflect more that differences in the extent of GPS tracking may be constitutionally significant in determining its intrusiveness. A few courts may go so far as to conclude that any use of GPS technology, even when attaching it, is presumptively unreasonable unless law enforcement first obtains a valid warrant.[72] Other courts may decide that the warrantless use of GPS technology is permissible, subject to one of the already settled warrant exceptions, such as when the suspect is fleeing and the police are engaged in hot pursuit. The state court decisions in Washington, Oregon, and New York seem to have adopted this approach under their own constitutions. Finally, some courts may argue, which could be seen as an attempt to reconcile the already existing decisions, that using GPS devices for a minimal amount of time—for a few days, perhaps—is permissible, but when the monitoring becomes prolonged—for many days, weeks, or months—the intrusiveness reaches a point where it becomes a search requiring a warrant.[73] The state court's decision in New York might also be read this way, and the D.C. Circuit appears to have followed this approach.[74]

COMPETING INTERESTS

In approaching warrantless use of GPS technology, courts confront the continued appropriateness of a principal corollary of Fourth Amendment doctrine. Fourth Amendment protection is premised on a reasonable expectation of privacy that society is willing to recognize. For decades, and in a variety of circumstances, courts have held that no privacy rights attach to activities that are visually observable to the public, such as movements along public streets. The pressure on this principle comes from the greatly enhanced reach and efficiency of tracking technologies such as GPS. Some contend that it would be better for legislatures rather than the courts to set the rules on GPS policy because they can more expressly balance the competing interests of enhancing law enforcement efficiency and protection of individual privacy.[75] Others argue that the courts are capable and equipped to do it, just as they have done reconciling the law to the usage of many other emerging technologies.[76]

Those who argue that law enforcement does not need to obtain a warrant to use GPS technology contend that the many uses of GPS technology simply "enable[] the police to be more effective in detecting crime,"[77] stamping it out at its earlier stages and preventing it from even occurring. Among others, the advantages in such technology, especially when police officers are engaged in a high-speed chase, decrease the likelihood of endangering the public, the police, or even the suspect from the potential hazards involved in such situations. Moreover, as already discussed, the efficiencies of GPS technology have enabled officers to prevent one woman from being raped and any further rapes from being committed by the suspect. Likewise, proponents of GPS use maintain that officers have been able to prevent drug production and distribution by the respective suspects they apprehended. GPS technology, then, can be preventive, saving lives and time; it decreases the cost of having officers out conducting surveillance while simultaneously allowing more places and people to be monitored and more action to be taken when criminal activity occurs. In short, from this perspective, GPS devices make law enforcement's job more efficient, safer, and effective, providing for a securer and safer society. They would argue that GPS technology functions "merely as an enhancing adjunct to the surveilling officer's eyes,"[78] and naked eye observation does not offend the Fourth Amendment because a person does not have a reasonable expectation of privacy in activity that any member of the public might observe. GPS technology is merely a matter of efficiency, they conclude, and the courts "have never equated police efficiency with unconstitutionality."[79]

Conversely, proponents of requiring law enforcement to obtain judicial permission before using a GPS device contend that efficiency, security, and safety come at some unacceptable costs.[80] At "the press of a button," for example, a GPS device can disclose one's activities that are "indisputably private [in] nature," such as "trips to the psychiatrist, the plastic surgeon, the abortion clinic, the AIDS treatment center, the strip club, the criminal defense attorney, the by-the-hour motel, the union meeting, the mosque, synagogue or church, the gay bar and on and on."[81] It does not only disclose "where we go, but by easy reference [it reveals] our associations—political, religious, amicable and amorous," as well as "the pattern of our professional and avocational pursuits."[82] GPS technology "is not a mere enhancement of human sensory capacity," because the information it can capture is potentially tantamount to, "at a minimum, millions of additional police officers and cameras on every street lamp."[83] A person does have a reasonable expectation of privacy from the government's ability to obtain such comprehensive and detailed information. The ability of the government to engage in monitoring that exposes this type of information, some even argue, foreshadows "Orwellian images of Big Brother secretly following your movements through the small device in your pocket"[84] or car, especially when the pervasive monitoring has been prolonged and continuous—for 28[85] and even 65[86] days, in certain cases. Besides, they contend, unless the situation is an emergency, it is not that onerous a burden to require the police to take a few minutes to obtain judicial approval before they use such revealing technology.[87]

CONCLUSION

Society's increased reliance on GPS technology raises both societal and legal considerations. Law enforcement has found many uses for GPS technology in criminal investigations. Some of these uses in connection with motor vehicle surveillance raise concerns over the technology's potential interference with privacy interests protected by the Fourth Amendment. Others have argued that GPS technology is comparable to naked eye observation, and its advantages in impeding and preventing criminal activity are substantial. However, others contend that balancing the privacy and law enforcement interests is not easy in a GPS context. There are also questions as to whether guidance of GPS use should be provided legislatively or judicially. It is important to note that the Fourth Amendment provides a floor for protection. No matter what the state legislatures or Congress does, the requirements of the Fourth Amendment must be met. Legislation provides two advantages: (1) clarification for procedural distinctions between warrantless and presumptively unreasonable searches, and (2) additional protection where reenforcement is thought necessary. Several state legislatures have enacted legislation governing the warrantless use of GPS devices. On the federal level, bills, such as S. 1212 and H.R. 2168, in part, delineate circumstances under which law enforcement may use, obtain, or disclose GPS information.

The Supreme Court is poised to speak to the use of GPS monitoring in Spring 2012 in *United States v. Jones*. State and lower federal courts have reached differing conclusions based on the facts presented, U.S. Supreme Court precedent on other tracking devices, and/or state constitutions.

End Notes

[1] Renee McDonald Hutchins, *Tied Up in Knotts? GPS Technology and the Fourth Amendment*, 55 UCLA L. Rev. 409, 414 (2007); *see also* the Global Positioning System, http://www.gps.gov.

[2] *See* Global Positioning System, Roads & Highways, http://www.gps.gov/applications/roads. One brand name example is a TomTom. The individual can enter into the device an address, and an automated voice, along with interactive maps, will guide the driver. *See* TomTom, How Does GPS Work?, http://www.tomtom.com/howdoesitwork/index.php?Language=1.

[3] *See, e.g.*, OnStar, Our Privacy Practices, Effective January 1, 2011, https://www.onstar.com/web/portal/privacy#Header. OnStar provides other limited circumstances when it will track the location of the vehicle, such as an in-car request for service, or when OnStar needs to conduct research or troubleshooting, it is delivering enhanced services, it is protecting its rights or the safety of the owner or others, or it is required to by law. *Id.*

[4] Adam Koppel, Note, *Warranting a Warrant: Fourth Amendment Concerns Raised by Law Enforcement's Warrantless Use of GPS and Cellular Tracking*, 64 U. Miami L. Rev. 1061, 1064 (2010).

[5] Joyce Priddy, *Different Uses of GPS Devices*, associatedcontent.com, (September 22, 2007), http://www.associatedcontent.com/article/389315/different_uses_of_gps_devices.html?cat=15; *see also* the Global Positioning System, Recreation, http://www.gps.gov/applications/recreation.

[6] The Global Positioning System, Timing, http://www.gps.gov/applications/timing.

[7] The Global Positioning System, Surveying & Mapping, http://www.gps.gov/applications/survey.

[8] The Global Positioning System, Aviation, http://www.gps.gov/applications/aviation.

[9] Koppel, *supra* note 4, at 1064 (providing statistics on the growing trends in GPS technology).

[10] The Global Positioning System, Public Safety & Disaster Relief, http://www.gps.gov/applications/safety.

[11] To illustrate the government's growing use of GPS technology in the area of criminal investigation, consider that "[i]n response to a Freedom of Information Act request, police in one Virginia locality reported that they used GPS devices in nearly 160 cases from 2005 to 2007." *Id.*

[12] Ben Hubbard, *Police Turn to Secret Weapon: GPS Device*, Wash. Post, A1 (August 13, 2008), available at http://www.washingtonpost.com/wpdyn/content/article/2008/08/12/AR2008081203275.html?nav=rss_metro/va; *see also* Ramya Shah, *From Beepers to GPS: Can the Fourth Amendment Keep Up with Electronic Tracking Technology?*, 2009 U. Ill. J.L. Tech. & Pol'y 281, 281 (Spring 2009) (providing an example of law enforcement's use of a GPS device to tie a suspect to the murder).

[13] *United States v. Garcia*, 474 F.3d 994, 995 (7th Cir. 2007).

[14] *People v. Weaver*, 909 N.E.2d 1195, 1195-96 (N.Y. 2009).

[15] Hutchins, *supra* note 1, at 418-19. The darts consist of a miniaturized GPS receiver, radio transmitter, and battery embedded in a sticky compound material.

[16] *Id.* at 419-20 (internal citations omitted).

[17] *Id.* at 419. Title III of the Omnibus Crime Control and Safe Streets Act of 1958 (P.L. 90-351) regulates the interception of wire, oral, and electronic communications. As such, it does not regulate the use of GPS technology affixed to vehicles and is beyond the scope of this report. For a discussion of wiretapping or electronic eavesdropping, refer to CRS Report 98-326, *Privacy: An Overview of Federal Statutes Governing Wiretapping and Electronic Eavesdropping*, by Gina Stevens and Charles Doyle.

[18] Michael Isikoff, *The Snitch in Your Pocket*, Newsweek (February 19, 2010), http://www.newsweek.com/2010/02/18/the-snitch-in-your-pocket.html.

[19] *Id.*

[20] Almost 50 years ago, in *Lopez v. United States*, 373 U.S. 427, 442 (1963), Chief Justice Warren remarked:

That the fantastic advances in the field of electronic communication constitute a great danger to the privacy of an individual; that indiscriminate use of such devices in law enforcement raises grave constitutional questions under the Fourth and Fifth Amendment;…"

[21] *See, e.g.*, Hutchins, *supra* note 1, at 464-65; Koppel, *supra* note 4, at 1089; *Maynard*, 615 F.3d at 564; *Weaver*,909 N.E.2d at 1201-02; Kip F. Wainscott, *Unwarranted Intrusion: GPS and the Fourth Amendment*, ACSblog (May 19, 2009, 11:52 AM), http://acslaw.org/node/13444?gclid=CLD254CK56QCFeFM5QodvBbU2A.

[22] *See, e.g.*, *Pineda-Moreno*, 591 F.3d at 1214-16; Tarik N. Jallad, Recent Development, *Old Answers to New Questions: GPS Surveillance and the Unwarranted Need for Warrants*, 11 N.C. J. L. & Tech. 351, 374-75 (Spring 2010); Orin Kerr, Does the Fourth Amendment Prohibit Warrantless GPS Surveillance?, The Volokh Conspiracy (Dec. 13, 2009), http://volokh.com/2009/12/13/does-the-fourth-amendment-prohibit-warrantless-gps-surveillance/.

[23] "The right of the people to be secure in their persons, houses, papers, and effects, against unreasonable searches and seizures, shall not be violated, and no Warrants shall issue, but upon probable cause, supported by Oath or affirmation, and particularly describing the place to be searched, and the persons or things to be seized." U.S. Const. amend. IV.

[24] This protection even includes searches and seizures conducted "beyond the sphere of criminal investigations." *City of Ontario v. Quon*, 130 S.Ct. 2619, 2627 (2010).

[25] Although the Fourth Amendment, like the Fifth Amendment, was originally understood to apply only to federal government action, *see Barron v. City of Baltimore*, 32 U.S. 243, 247-51 (1833), the Supreme Court later found that it became applicable to the states through the Due Process Clause of the Fourteenth Amendment. *Mapp v. Ohio*, 367 U.S.643, 660 (1961).

[26] Garcia, 474 F.3d at 996.

[27] *See, e.g.*, *City of Ontario*, 130 S.Ct. at 2630; *Brigham City v. Stuart*, 547 U.S. 398, 403 (2006); *Groh v. Ramirez*, 540 U.S. 551, 559 (2004); *United States v. Ross*, 456 U.S. 798, 824-25 (1982); *Mincey v. Arizona*, 437 U.S. 385, 390 (1978); *Katz v. United States*, 389 U.S. 347, 357 (1967). The Court has gone back and forth on whether warrantless searches or seizures are presumptively unreasonable or per se unreasonable. It is unclear which approach the Court currently follows.

[28] *Brigham City*, 547 U.S. at 403. As the Court in *Brigham City* outlined, some of these exceptions include law enforcement's engaging "in hot pursuit of a fleeing suspect," preventing "the imminent destruction of evidence," extinguishing a fire on private property and investigating its cause, or assisting "persons who are seriously injured or threatened with such injury." *Id.* (internal quotations and citations omitted).

[29] *See, e.g.*, *Boyd v. United States*, 116 U.S. 616, 627 (1886); *Adams v. New York*, 192 U.S. 585, 598 (1904); *Olmstead v. United States*, 277 U.S. 438, 464-66 (1928); *Goldman v. United States*, 316 U.S. 129, 134-36 (1942); *see also Kyllo v. United States*, 533 U.S. 27, 31-33 (2001) (discussing the historical evolving emphasis of Fourth Amendment protection).

[30] *See, e.g., Silverthorne Lumber Co. v. United States*, 251 U.S. 385 (1920); *Jones v. United States*, 362 U.S. 257, 266 (1960), *overruled on other grounds by United States v. Salvucci*, 448 U.S. 83 (1980); *Silverman v. United States*, 365 U.S. 505, 511-12 (1961); *Warden v. Hayden*, 387 U.S. 294, 304 (1967); *Rakas v. Illinois*, 439 U.S. 128, 143 (1986).

[31] *Warden*, 387 U.S. at 304-05 (discussing the shift of emphasis from property to privacy).

[32] *Katz*, 389 U.S. at 353. This focus finds support in the Amendment's text, which begins by stating that it protects"[t]he right of the people." U.S. Const. amend. IV.

[33] 389 U.S. 347 (1967).

[34] *Kyllo*, 533 U.S. at 33 (quoting *Katz*, 389 U.S. at 353).

[35] The Fourth Amendment's mandates are enforced through the application of an exclusionary rule which generally states that evidence illegally seized may not be used against the defendant. *See, Weeks v. United States*, 232 U.S. 383 (1914) (holding that the Fourth Amendment barred the use of evidence secured through a warrantless search); *Mapp v.Ohio*, 367 U.S. 643 (1961) (holding that the exclusionary rule applies to the states).

[36] *Kyllo*, 533 U.S. at 32. "A search," the Court has explained, "comprises the individual interest in privacy; a seizure deprives the individual of dominion over his or her [person or] personal property." *Horton v. California*, 496 U.S. 128,133 (1990). The use of a GPS to conduct surveillance would seem to fall under the rubric of a search; the attachment ofa GPS device lends itself more to the concept of a seizure. *See United States v. Karo*, 468 U.S. 705, 712-13 (1984)(recognizing the difference in issues raised by the two concepts).

[37] *California v. Greenwood*, 486 U.S. 35, 40-41 (1988).

[38] *United States v. Ciraolo*, 476 U.S. 207, 211 (1986) (quoting *Katz v. United States*, 389 U.S. 347, 360 (1967) (Harlan, J., concurring)); see also Kyllo, 533 U.S. at 33-34.

[39] *Ciraolo*, 476 U.S. at 211; *see also Kyllo*, 533 U.S. at 34.

[40] 533 U.S. 27, 34 (2001).

[41] 476 U.S. 207, 213-15 (1986).

[42] 460 U.S. 276, 281-84 (1983).

[43] However, the Court found that the arrest warrant was valid, as it was based on an affidavit, which contained a significant amount of evidence from sources other than the beeper.

[44] 468 U.S. 705, 713-16 (1984).

[45] *But see*, 468 U.S. at 729-30 (Stevens, J., dissenting) (stating that the beeper's attachment constituted a "seizure.").

[46] The Court declined to decide whether a search warrant to monitor a beeper would require probable cause or reasonable suspicion.

[47] *United States v. Maynard*, 615 F.3d 544, 564 (D.C. Cir. 2010)(listing several states and the relevant legislation in each). *See, e.g.*, Utah Code Ann. §§ 77-23a-4, 77-23a-7, 77-23a-15.5; Minn. Stat. §§ 626A.37, 626A.35; Fla. Stat. §§ 934.06, 934.42; S.C.Code Ann. § 17-30-140; Okla. Stat., tit. 13, §§ 176.6, 177.6; Haw. Rev. Stat. §§ 803-42, 803-44.7; 18 Pa. Cons.Stat. § 5761.

[48] *See State v. Weaver*, 909 N.E.2d 1195 (N.Y. 2009) (GPS use, under state constitution, is unconstitutional without a warrant); *State v. Jackson*, 76 P.3d 217 (Wash. 2003); *State v. Campbell*, 759 P.2d 1040 (Or. 1988); *Delaware v. Biddle*, No. CRIM.A. 05-01-1052, 2005 WL 3073593, at *1 (Del. Com. Pl. May 5, 2005); *see also Commonwealth v. Connolly*, 913 N.E.2d 356 (Mass. 2009) (installation of a GPS device was a seizure).

[49] 909 N.E.2d 1195 (N.Y. 2009).

[50] *Id.* at 1202.

[51] *Id.*

[52] *See Osburn v. State*, 44 P.3d 523 (Nev. 2002); *Foltz v. Commonwealth*, 698 S.E.2d 281 (Va. Ct. App. 2010), *reh'g en banc granted and mandate stayed by* 699 S.E. 2d 522 (Va. Ct. App. 2010).

[53] 698 S.E.3d 281 (Va. Ct. App. 2010), *reh'g en banc granted and mandate stayed by* 699 S.E. 2d 522 (Va. Ct. App.2010).

[54] *Id.* at 286.

[55] *See, e.g., United States v. Garcia*, 474 F.3d 994 (7th Cir. 2007); *United States v. Marquez*, 605 F.3d 604 (8th Cir. 2010); *United States v. Pineda-Moreno*, 591 F.3d 1212 (9th Cir. 2010); *United States v. Eberle*, 993 F.Supp. 794 (D. Mont. 1998); *United States v. Moran*, 349 F. Supp. 2d 425 (N.D.N.Y.2005); *United States v. Burton*, 698 F. Supp. 2d 1303 (N.D. Fl. 2010); *United States v. Williams*, 650 F. Supp. 2d 633 (W.D. KY. 2009); *United States v. Jesus-Nunez*, No. 1:10-CR-00017-01, 2010 WL 2991229, at *1 (July 27, 2010).

[56] 591 F.3d 1212 (9th Cir. 2010).

[57] *Id.* at 1213.

[58] *Id.*

[59] *Id.* at 1214.

[60] *Id.* at 1214-15.

[61] *Id.* at 1216.

[62] *Id.* at 1216-17 (quoting *Knotts*, 460 U.S. at 284) (alterations in original).

[63] *Knotts*, 460 U.S. at 284.

[64] *Pineda-Moreno*, 591 F.3d at 1216 n.2 (quoting *Garcia*, 474 F.3d at 998).

[65] *United States v. Maynard*, 615 F.3d 544 (D.C. Cir. 2010). This was a consolidated case with two defendants, Jones and Maynard. The D.C. Circuit Court of Appeals reversed Jones's conviction but affirmed Maynard's. The government appealed Jones's reversal. As such, the case before the Supreme Court is *United States v. Jones*.

[66] *Id.*

[67] *Id.* at 558.

[68] *Id.* at 567.

[69] *Id.* at 556-58 ("In short, *Knotts* held only that '[a] person traveling in an automobile on public thoroughfares has no reasonable expectation of privacy in his movements from one place to another,' not that such a person has no reasonable expectation of privacy in his movements whatsoever, world without end.").

[70] *Id.* at 558-67.

[71] The D.C. Circuit Court of Appeals reversed Jones's conviction but affirmed Maynard's. The government appealed Jones's reversal. As such, the case before the Supreme Court is *United States v. Jones*, 131 S.Ct. 3064 (2011).

[72] *See, e.g., Connolly*, 913 N.E.2d at 822.

[73] This approach could be called the "Mosaic Theory." The idea is that when GPS surveillance is prolonged, the sum of otherwise publicly exposed activities reveals patterns that are reasonably expected to be private, thus constituting a search, which requires a warrant. *See* Orin Kerr, *D.C. Circuit Introduces "Mosaic Theory" of Fourth Amendment, Holds GPS Monitoring a Fourth Amendment Search*, The Volokh Conspiracy (August 6, 2010), http://volokh.com/2010/08/06/d-c-circuit-introduces-mosaic-theory-of-fourth-amendment-holds-gps-monitoring-a-fourth-amendment-search/. The court in *Maynard* used this theory and tied it to the Supreme Court's dragnet reservation in *Knotts*. However, unlike the 9th and 7th Circuits, the D.C. Circuit read it to apply when law enforcement engages in prolonged surveillance, not just mass surveillance. *Maynard*, 615 F.3d at 557-63.

[74] The United States petitioned for a rehearing *en banc* to the court's decision in *Maynard*. Orin Kerr, *DOJ Petitions for Rehearing in DC Circuit "Mosaic Theory" GPS Surveillance Case*, The Volokh Conspiracy (September 22, 2010), http://volokh.com/2010/09/22/doj-petitions-for-rehearing-in-dc-circuit-mosaic-theory-gps-surveillance-case/.

[75] Orin S. Kerr, *The Fourth Amendment and New Technologies: Constitutional Myths and the Case for Caution*, 102 Mich. L. Rev. 801, 806 (2004).

[76] *See generally* Hutchins, supra note 1; *see also* Renee McDonald Hutchins, *The Anatomy of a Search: Intrusiveness and the Fourth Amendment*, 44 U. Rich. L. Rev. 1185, 1189 n.22 (May 2010) (noting the current debate between whether the legislature or the judiciary is the preferred arbiter in the area of GPS technology).

[77] *Pineda-Moreno*, 591 F.3d at 1216 (quoting *Knotts*, 460 U.S. at 284).

[78] *Weaver*, 909 N.E.2d at 1199.

[79] *Knotts*, 460 U.S. at 284.

[80] Some cite, for example, an Historical Review of the Constitution and Government of Pennsylvania, title page (1759) (Arno Press reprint 1972) (stating that "[t]hose who would give up essential Liberty, to purchase a little temporary Safety, deserve neither Liberty nor Safety") (commonly attributed to Benjamin Franklin).

[81] *Weaver*, 909 N.E. 2d at 1198-99.

[82] *Id.*

[83] *Id.*

[84] Michael Isikoff, *The Snitch in Your Pocket*, Newsweek, February 19, 2010, available at http:// www.newsweek.com/ 2010/02/18/the-snitch-in-your-pocket.html; *see also Pineda-Moreno*, 617 F.3d 1120, 1121, 1126 (9th Cir. 2010) (Kozinski, C.J., dissenting from the denial of rehearing en banc).

[85] *Maynard*, 615 F.3d at 558.

[86] *Weaver*, 909 N.E 2d at 1195.

[87] "[O]fficers in Utah can get electronic warrants in about 20 minutes. 'It's not that hard,'" a Utah County Sherriff stated. Janice Peterson, *Conflicting views on no-warrant GPS ruling*, Daily Herald (September 5, 2010), available at http://www.heraldextra.com/news/local/article_6d44220a-e8d1-5d0b-a072-bce72e97a835.html.

In: The Fourth Amendment
Editor: Lucille E. Huff
ISBN: 978-1-63321-634-1

Chapter 5

DRONES IN DOMESTIC SURVEILLANCE OPERATIONS: FOURTH AMENDMENT IMPLICATIONS AND LEGISLATIVE RESPONSES*

Richard M. Thompson II

SUMMARY

The prospect of drone use inside the United States raises far-reaching issues concerning the extent of government surveillance authority, the value of privacy in the digital age, and the role of Congress in reconciling these issues.

Drones, or unmanned aerial vehicles (UAVs), are aircraft that can fly without an onboard human operator. An unmanned aircraft system (UAS) is the entire system, including the aircraft, digital network, and personnel on the ground. Drones can fly either by remote control or on a predetermined flight path; can be as small as an insect and as large as a traditional jet; can be produced more cheaply than traditional aircraft; and can keep operators out of harm's way. These unmanned aircraft are most commonly known for their operations overseas in tracking down and killing suspected members of Al Qaeda and related organizations. In addition to these missions abroad, drones are being considered for use in

---

* This is an edited, reformatted and augmented version of a Congressional Research Service publication, No. R42701, dated April 3, 2013.

domestic surveillance operations to protect the homeland, assist in crime fighting, disaster relief, immigration control, and environmental monitoring.

Although relatively few drones are currently flown over U.S. soil, the Federal Aviation Administration (FAA) predicts that 30,000 drones will fill the nation's skies in less than 20 years. Congress has played a large role in this expansion. In February 2012, Congress enacted the FAA Modernization and Reform Act (P.L. 112-95), which calls for the FAA to accelerate the integration of unmanned aircraft into the national airspace system by 2015. However, some Members of Congress and the public fear there are insufficient safeguards in place to ensure that drones are not used to spy on American citizens and unduly infringe upon their fundamental privacy. These observers caution that the FAA is primarily charged with ensuring air traffic safety, and is not adequately prepared to handle the issues of privacy and civil liberties raised by drone use.

This report assesses the use of drones under the Fourth Amendment right to be free from unreasonable searches and seizures. The touchstone of the Fourth Amendment is reasonableness. A reviewing court's determination of the reasonableness of a drone search would likely be informed by location of the search, the sophistication of the technology used, and society's conception of privacy in an age of rapid technological advancement. While individuals can expect substantial protections against warrantless government intrusions into their homes, the Fourth Amendment offers less robust restrictions upon government surveillance occurring in public places including areas immediately outside the home, such as in driveways or backyards. Concomitantly, as technology advances, the contours of what is reasonable under the Fourth Amendment may adjust as people's expectations of privacy evolve.

In the 113th Congress, several measures have been introduced that would restrict the use of drones at home. Several of the bills would require law enforcement to obtain a warrant before using drones for domestic surveillance, subject to several exceptions. Others would establish a regime under which the drone user must file a data collection statement stating when, where, how the drone will be used and how the user will minimize the collection of information protected by the legislation.

INTRODUCTION

The prospect of drone use in domestic surveillance operations has engendered considerable debate among Americans of various political ideologies.[1]

Opponents of drone surveillance have complained that the use of unmanned aircraft on American soil infringes upon fundamental privacy interests and the ability to freely associate with others.[2] Some are specifically concerned about the possibility of turning military technology inward to surveil American citizens.[3] Proponents have responded by emphasizing their potential benefits, which may include protecting public safety, patrolling our nation's borders, and investigating and enforcing environmental and criminal law violations.[4]

The tension between security and privacy interests is not new, but has been heightened by the explosion of surveillance technology in recent decades. Police officers who were once relegated to naked eye observations may soon have, or in some cases already possess, the capability to see through walls or track an individual's movements from the sky.[5] One might question, then: What is the proper balance between the necessity of the government to keep people safe and the privacy needs of individuals? As some polls suggest, while the public supports drone usage in certain circumstances, they are less enthusiastic about using them as part of routine law enforcement activity.[6]

The Fourth Amendment to the United States Constitution safeguards Americans' privacy and prevents excessive government intrusion by prohibiting "unreasonable searches and seizures."[7] Courts have long grappled with how to apply the text of this 18th century provision to 20th century technologies.

Although the Supreme Court has the final say in the interpretation of the Fourth Amendment and other constitutional safeguards,[8] Congress and, in many cases, the President are free to institute more stringent restrictions upon government surveillance operations.[9]

This report first explores the potential uses of drones in the domestic sphere by federal, state, and local governments. It then surveys current Fourth Amendment jurisprudence, including cases surrounding privacy in the home, privacy in public spaces, location tracking, manned aerial surveillance, and those involving the national border.

Next, it considers how existing jurisprudence may inform current and proposed drone uses. It then describes the various legislative measures introduced in the 113th Congress to address the legal and policy issues surrounding drones. Finally, it briefly identifies several alternative approaches that may constrain the potential scope of drone surveillance.

Background, Uses, and Drone Technology

Drones, also known as unmanned aerial vehicles (UAVs), are aircraft that do not carry a human operator and are capable of flight under remote control or autonomous programming.[10] An unmanned aircraft system (UAS) is the entire system, including the aircraft, digital network, and personnel on the ground.[11] Drones can range from the size of an insect—sometimes called nano drones or micro UAVs—to the size of a traditional jet.[12]

Drones are perhaps most commonly recognized from their missions abroad, including to target and kill suspected members of Al Qaeda and related groups, but they might be used for a variety of other purposes, including for both commercial and law enforcement activities within the United States. In fact, the FAA predicted that 30,000 unmanned aircraft could be flying in U.S. skies in less than 20 years.[13] One reason for this expansion has been a push by Congress for a faster integration of UAVs into U.S. airspace.[14] Most recently, as part of the FAA Modernization and Reform Act of 2012, Congress mandated that the Federal Aviation Administration (FAA) "develop a comprehensive plan to safely accelerate the integration of civil unmanned aircraft systems into the national airspace system."[15] This plan shall provide for integration of UAVs by September 2015.

Drones have been employed domestically by federal, state, and local governments in a range of circumstances. The Department of Homeland Security (DHS) uses them to police the nation's borders to deter unlawful border crossings by unauthorized aliens, criminals, and terrorists, and to detect and interdict the smuggling of weapons, drugs, and other contraband into the country.[16] Within DHS, Customs and Border Protection's (CBP's) Office of Air and Marine (OAM) has flown missions to support federal and state agencies such as the Federal Bureau of Investigation (FBI), the Department of Defense (DOD), Immigration and Customs Enforcement (ICE), the U.S. Secret Service, and the Texas Rangers.[17] According to a recent disclosure by the FAA, several local police departments, state and private colleges, and small cities and towns have also received FAA Certificates of Authorization (COAs) to fly unmanned aircraft domestically.[18] Recently, a police force in North Dakota conducted the nation's first drone-assisted arrest.[19] DHS, in conjunction with local law enforcement agencies, has been testing drone capabilities in a host of other situations including detecting radiation, monitoring a hostage situation, tracking a gun tossed by a fleeing suspect, firefighting, and finding missing persons.[20]

Currently, drones can be outfitted with high-powered cameras,[21] thermal imaging devices,[22] license plate readers,[23] and laser radar (LADAR).[24] In the near future, law enforcement organizations might seek to outfit drones with facial recognition or soft biometric recognition, which can recognize and track individuals based on attributes such as height, age, gender, and skin color.[25] As explained below, the relative sophistication of drones contrasted with traditional surveillance technology may influence a court's decision whether domestic drone use is lawful under the Fourth Amendment.

FOURTH AMENDMENT "SEARCH" JURISPRUDENCE

The Fourth Amendment's story is one of continuity and change. Core values such as privacy and protection from excessive and arbitrary government intrusion are always within its sweep. A continuing question, though, is how the demands of its protection apply to an ever-changing society in which new and pervasive forms of technology are increasingly common. Although there are numerous rules and exceptions throughout the Supreme Court's Fourth Amendment jurisprudence, this section will explore those most pertinent to domestic drone use.

In short, the Fourth Amendment regulates when, where, and how the government may conduct searches and seizures. The Amendment provides, in relevant part: "The right of the people to be secure in their persons, houses, papers, and effects, against unreasonable searches and seizures, shall not be violated[.]"[26] The Fourth Amendment does not apply to all government acts, but only to those that constitute a search. So when does government monitoring constitute a Fourth Amendment "search" for which a warrant is generally required? Initially, courts' assessment focused on the specific area being investigated. Consider the 1928 case *Olmstead v. United States*.[27] There, the Supreme Court held that police wiretaps of the defendant's home telephone did not constitute a Fourth Amendment search because the police did not trespass onto Olmstead's property to intercept his conversation.[28] The Court's thinking at the time was that if the person's home, tangible property, or papers were not physically invaded, then no search in the constitutional sense occurred. Almost 40 years later, the Court shifted focus from property to privacy interests.[29] In *Katz v. United States*, decided in 1967, the Court held that an FBI agent's use of a bug to listen to the private conversations of Mr. Katz while in a telephone booth violated his Fourth Amendment rights.[30] Although he was in a public telephone booth and there was no physical invasion, the Court noted that what a person "seeks to preserve private, even in an area accessible to the public, may be constitutionally protected."[31] One of the modern Fourth Amendment tests relied upon by courts in assessing whether government monitoring constitutes a "search" derives from Justice Harlan's concurrence in *Katz*. It considers whether the person has a subjective expectation of privacy in the area to be searched and whether society is prepared to deem that expectation reasonable.[32]

Although the Court said in *Katz* that the Fourth Amendment "protects people not places,"[33] Justice Harlan noted that determining what "protection it affords people ... requires reference to a '*place*.'"[34] And as Justice Scalia observed when writing for a majority of the Court in *United States v. Jones*, a Fourth Amendment search occurs, "at a minimum," where "the Government obtains information by physically intruding on a constitutionally protected area."[35] The majority in *Jones* indicated that the reasonable expectation of privacy test was never intended to replace the property-based approach used in earlier cases, but merely augment it.[36] So where do individuals enjoy the most Fourth Amendment protection? The least? Why does the location dictate the level of protection? And how does technology affect society's expectation of privacy?

When analyzing domestic drone use under the Fourth Amendment, a reviewing court may be informed by cases surrounding privacy in the home, privacy in public spaces, location tracking, manned aerial surveillance, those involving the national border, and warrantless searches under the special needs doctrine.

Privacy in the Home

The home has always held a central place in American life, and remains the area accorded the greatest Fourth Amendment protection.[37] The Fourth Amendment protects this zone of privacy by ensuring that "the right of the people to be secure in their ... houses ... against unreasonable search and seizure, shall not be violated[.]"[38] In most instances, the Supreme Court has rigorously adhered to this safeguard.[39] For instance, although police officers may make a warrantless arrest of an individual for a felony offense committed in public,[40] they may not step inside his home without a warrant, barring any recognized exception.[41]

In addition to a physical entry and search of the home, police are likewise prohibited from using certain technology to pierce this zone of privacy. In

Kyllo v. United States, government agents used a thermal-imaging device to determine heat patterns inside the home of Danny Kyllo.[42] The Court began with the presumption that a warrantless search of a home is unreasonable.[43] Ultimately, the Court protected this "realm of guaranteed privacy" by holding that obtaining information about the inside of a home that could not otherwise be obtained except by entering the home, through the use of technology not in "general public use," is a "search" covered by the Fourth Amendment.[44]

The home, however, does not provide an absolute shield against government surveillance. As Justice Harlan emphasized in *Katz*, "[A] man's home is, for most purposes, a place where he expects privacy, but objects, activities, or statements that he exposes to the plain view of outsiders are not 'protected' because no intention to keep them to himself has been exhibited." Indeed, in certain instances, police may use their natural senses to conduct warrantless searches of the inside of a home.[45] To fall under this exception—known as the "plain view" doctrine—the police must be in a lawful vantage point when they conduct the surveillance, and the incriminating nature of the evidence must be readily apparent.[46]

Curtilage and Open Fields

Once an individual moves from the confines of the home, he is entitled to different Fourth Amendment considerations. Depending on a host of varying factors, areas outside of the home may be considered "curtilage" or "open fields."[47] The curtilage is the area immediately surrounding the home—an area the Court has granted similar protections as the inside of the home.[48] To determine if an area is curtilage, a court will look at how close the area is to the home; whether the area is within a fence surrounding the home; how the area is used; and whether the area is protected from observation by passersby.[49] Although an area may be deemed curtilage—as with the home—it is not veiled with unconditional constitutional protection. As the Court noted in one aerial surveillance case:

> The Fourth Amendment protection of the home has never been extended to require law enforcement officers to shield their eyes when passing by a home on public thoroughfares. Nor does the mere fact that an individual has taken measures to restrict some views of his activities preclude an officer's observations from a public vantage point where he has a right to be and which renders the activities clearly visible.[50]

On the other hand, the area outside the curtilage is sometimes considered "open fields," which "do not provide the setting for those intimate activities that the Amendment is intended to shelter from governmental interference or surveillance,"[51] and thus are not given similar Fourth Amendment protections. Differentiating between the two is no easy task. In one case, for example, the Ninth Circuit Court of Appeals determined that the defendant's driveway was not curtilage as he had taken no affirmative steps to block it from observation by passers-by.[52] Furthermore, in the fly-over cases discussed *infra*, the Supreme Court has permitted similar searches in both open fields and the curtilage, to some extent eliminating any constitutional difference between the two.

Manned Aerial Surveillance

In a series of cases that provide the closest analogy to UAVs, the Supreme Court addressed the use of *manned* aircraft to conduct domestic surveillance over residential and industrial areas. In each, the Court held that the fly-over at issue was not a search prohibited by the Fourth Amendment, as the areas surveilled were open to public view.

In *California v. Ciraolo*, police received a tip that an individual was growing marijuana in his backyard next to his suburban home.[54] Because two fences blocked their view of the yard, officers flew a fixed-wing aircraft at an altitude of 1,000 feet over the property to conduct a visual inspection. From this vantage point, the officers readily identified with the naked eye marijuana plants growing in the defendant's yard. The Court held that the defendant's expectation of privacy in the area immediately surrounding his home was not reasonable, since "what a person knowingly exposes to the public ... is not a subject of Fourth Amendment protection."[55] "Any member of the public flying in this airspace who glanced down could have seen everything these officers observed," the Court remarked.[56] Much weight was placed on the fact that the plane was at all times in navigable airspace as defined by federal statute.[57]

Similarly, in *Florida v. Riley*, local police received a tip that an individual was growing marijuana in a greenhouse located 10 to 20 feet away from his mobile home.[58] The officers could not see the contents of the greenhouse from the ground, so they flew a helicopter over the defendant's backyard at an altitude of 400 feet. While overhead, an officer saw marijuana plants through a crack in the greenhouse roof. Because the helicopter, like the plane in *Ciraolo*, was in navigable airspace—where any member of the public could have flown—the Court did not consider this a search for which a warrant was required.[59]

> "What a person knowingly exposes to the public ... is not a subject of Fourth Amendment protection."[53]

In the final case of the series, *Dow Chemical v. United States*, the Court was asked whether a theory of "industrial curtilage" would prevent a government agency from conducting aerial surveillance over a 2,000-acre commercial plant.[60] There, after Dow Chemical Co. refused access to the Environmental Protection Agency (EPA), the EPA hired a commercial aerial photographer to take photos of the facility using a precision aerial mapping camera. Having ruled out the argument that the areas surrounding an industrial complex are entitled to the same protection as similar areas surrounding a home, the Court concluded that photographing the plant from navigable airspace was not a search.[61]

Government Tracking

Like the aerial surveillance cases, individuals have reduced—and in some contexts no—Fourth Amendment protection from government tracking of their travel in public places. This has permitted the government to conduct warrantless tracking of a vehicle's movements while traveling on public streets. However, once people enter a private residence, the tracking must cease. Also, using technology to perform pervasive tracking might not meet Fourth Amendment muster.

Consider, for example, these two government tracking cases, *United States v. Knotts* and *United States v. Karo*.[62] In both cases, the government hid a location monitoring device in an item that was then given to the suspects. In *Knotts*, the police tracked the suspect's movements solely while traveling on public roadways.[63] The Court held that people have no reasonable expectation of privacy in their movements on public streets. As such, no Fourth Amendment search occurred, thus no warrant was required. By contrast, in *Karo*, the police tracked a beeper device on public streets *and* while the beeper was in a private residence—a "location not open to visual surveillance."[64] "Indiscriminate monitoring of property that has been withdrawn from public view," the Court declared, "would present far too serious a threat to privacy interests in the home to escape entirely some sort of Fourth Amendment oversight."[65] The Court held the search unlawful.

Although surveillance in public is generally not considered a search, pervasive tracking may cross the line. Take, for instance, the Supreme Court's recent decision in the GPS tracking case *United States v. Jones.*[66] In that case, the Court held that the attachment and monthlong tracking of a GPS device on an individual's vehicle constituted a trespass, and hence a Fourth Amendment search.[67] The Court grounded its decision in the property-based approach to assessing what constitutes a "search" under the Fourth Amendment, which had been more prevalent in the late 19th and early 20th century cases involving relatively unsophisticated technology.

The Court's focus on whether the attachment of a tracking device constitutes a trespass triggering Fourth Amendment protections is not necessarily applicable to drone surveillance. However, in two separate concurring opinions that together made up five members of the Court, an alternative framework was proposed that may have more far-reaching implications for the domestic use of UAVs.

Justice Alito, concurring in the Court's judgment, and joined by Justices Ginsburg, Breyer, and Kagan, would have held that "the use of longer term GPS monitoring in investigations of most offenses impinges on expectations of privacy. For such offenses, society's expectation has been that law enforcement agents and others would not— and indeed, in the main, simply could not—secretly monitor and catalogue every single movement of an individual's car for a very long period." Justice Sotomayor, joining the controlling opinion in *Jones*, but also concurring separately, noted that although following people for a short period of time conveys little information about them, tracking an individual for an extended period "reflects a wealth of detail about her familial, political, professional, religious, and sexual associations."[69] Thus, the length of time an individual is kept under surveillance and the breadth of data collected through such surveillance may inform a reviewing court whether a particular surveillance practice constitutes a Fourth Amendment search.[70]

Tracking an individual for an extended period "reflects a wealth of detail about her familial, political, professional, religious, and sexual associations."[68]

Border Searches

Even more so than surveillance of public places generally, law enforcement agencies are granted significant deference to conduct surveillance at or near American borders. The federal government has a significant interest in protecting American borders from crossings by persons attempting to enter unlawfully, drug trafficking, and, perhaps most importantly, the transit of weapons and persons seeking to do harm to American people and infrastructure.

Congress has granted federal law enforcement agencies significant search powers at the border. Section 287 of the Immigration and Nationality Act (INA), codified at 8 U.S.C. Section 1357, authorizes immigration officers to conduct warrantless searches of any vessel within a reasonable distance from the United States border and any vehicle within 25 miles from a border for the "purpose of patrolling the border to prevent the illegal entry of aliens into the United States."[71] Similarly, 19 U.S.C. Section 482 authorizes customs officers to search vehicles and persons on which or whom they have reasonable cause to believe are carrying goods unlawfully into the United States.[72]

The Supreme Court has likewise acknowledged this federal interest in the borders, observing that "[t]he Government's interest in preventing the entry of unwanted persons and effects is at its zenith at the international border."[73] Again, the touchstone in every Fourth Amendment case is whether the search is *reasonable*.[74] The Court observed in *United States v. Montoya De Hernandez* that "the Fourth Amendment balance of reasonableness is qualitatively different at the international border."[75] "Routine searches," the Court continued, "are not subject to any requirement of reasonable suspicion, probable cause, or warrant."[76] "Routine" searches have included pat downs for weapons or contraband,[77] the use of drug sniffing dogs,[78] and the inspection of luggage.[79] By contrast, "non-routine" searches are those that go beyond a limited intrusion, and require the government official to have (at a minimum) "reasonable suspicion" of wrongdoing.[80] Prolonged detentions,[81] strip searches,[82] and body cavity searches[83] have all been considered non-routine searches.

Unlike searches directly at the border, the Court has shown more reticence in granting law enforcement unfettered discretion to conduct searches near, but not directly at, the border. In *Almeida-Sanchez v. United States*, the defendant's vehicle was stopped and searched by U.S. Border Patrol agents 25 miles north of the U.S.-Mexico border.[84] The agents had neither a warrant nor probable cause, nor even reasonable suspicion, to conduct the search. The government argued that the search was permissible under Section 287 of the Immigration and Nationality Act. A federal statute, the Court noted, cannot trump the Constitution. The Court refused to permit this suspicionless search, as it was conducted neither at the border nor at its "functional equivalent."[85]

Warrants, Suspicionless Searches, and Special Needs

The baseline rule in Fourth Amendment cases is that police must obtain a warrant to search an individual or their property in all but a few limited instances.[86] This rule ensures that an independent judicial officer, rather than a police officer in the field, is determining whether there is probable cause to conduct a search or seizure.[87] Over time, however, the Court has loosened this warrant requirement in instances where a strict showing of individualized suspicion of probable cause would hinder the government from addressing health and safety concerns.[88] In two lines of overlapping cases—administrative searches and "special needs" cases—the Court has balanced the individual's privacy interest against the government's interest to determine if a warrant or any individualized suspicion is required.[89] These two theories permit law enforcement to conduct dragnet searches in certain instances.

Suspicionless general searches are ones "in which the government searches or seizes every person, place, or thing in a specific location or involved in a specific activity based only on a showing of a generalized government interest."[90] Suspicionless searches have been conducted at the national border,[91] private businesses,[92] and police roadblocks.[93] In the roadblock cases, the Court has balanced the government's interest against the individual's privacy interest to determine whether police may stop and question drivers without a warrant or any suspicion of criminal wrongdoing. In *Michigan Dep't of State Police v. Sitz*, the Court upheld the suspicionless stopping and examination of drivers for intoxication at sobriety checkpoints.[94] The Court reasoned that the high incidence of drunk driving balanced against the minimal intrusion on drivers permitted suspicionless checkpoints. In *City of Indianapolis v. Edmund*, however, law enforcement was not permitted to set up a drug interdiction checkpoint.[95] The Court held that searches such as this violated the Fourth Amendment when their "primary purpose" is "to uncover evidence of ordinary criminal wrongdoing."[96] Justice O'Connor observed that if this type of roadblock were allowed "the Fourth Amendment would do little to prevent such intrusions from becoming a routine part of American life."[97]

Application of Fourth Amendment to Drone Surveillance

As evidenced by the foregoing, the constitutionality of domestic drone surveillance may depend upon the context in which such surveillance takes place. Whether a targeted individual is at home, in his backyard, in the public square, or near a national border will play a large role in determining whether he is entitled to privacy. Equally important is the sophistication of the technology used by law enforcement and the duration of the surveillance. Both of these factors will likely inform a reviewing court's reasoning as to whether the government's surveillance constitutes an unreasonable search in violation of the Fourth Amendment.

Location of Search

Based on existing case law, it is reasonable to assume that surveillance of an individual while in his home—an area accorded the greatest Fourth Amendment protection—using technology not in general public use would be an unlawful search absent a search warrant. The Supreme Court in *Kyllo* was particularly concerned about law enforcement's use of powerful equipment to peer inside an individual's home. Currently, UAVs carry high-megapixel cameras and thermal imaging, and will soon have the capacity to see through walls and ceilings.[98] These technologies are not generally available to the public, and under current jurisprudence, their use by law enforcement would probably constitute a search covered by the Fourth Amendment. However, the use of low-powered cameras or other unsophisticated technology to view people and objects in plain view while in their home might not trigger Fourth Amendment protections. The rationale for this notion is that officers are not required to avert their eyes when they see illegal activity in plain view, especially when the subject of the search has taken no affirmative efforts to hide their activity from public view.

Moving beyond the home, it is unclear whether circumstances exist in which the area immediately surrounding the home—for instance, a backyard, a swimming pool, a deck, or a porch—would receive similar protections as the interior of the home if surveilled by drones or other aerial vehicles.[99] Although the Supreme Court has recited on many occasions that a person located in a home's curtilage is accorded similar privacy protections as when inside the home, the aerial surveillance cases arguably constitute an exception to this general principle. In the two aerial cases, *Riley* and *Ciraolo*, the area surveilled was within close proximity of the home, yet the police surveillance at altitudes of 400 and 1,000 feet were not considered a search.

Based on the aerial surveillance cases, it may be reasonable to presume a warrant would *not* be required (nor, perhaps, any suspicion, for that matter) to conduct drone surveillance of most public places for a relatively short period of time. The Supreme Court remarked in *Ciraolo* that the "Fourth Amendment simply does not require the police traveling in the public airways at [1,000 feet] to obtain a warrant to observe what is visible to the naked eye."[100] However, the rarity of drone flights may distinguish their use from surveillance by the piloted aircraft used in the three aerial cases decided by the Court. All three of these cases were premised on the fact that each aircraft was flying in navigable airspace, and that these flights were not "sufficiently rare" to provide a reasonable expectation of privacy in the area to be searched. To this point, Justice White remarked in *Riley* that "there is nothing in the record or before us to suggest that helicopters flying at 400 feet are sufficiently rare in this country to lend substance to respondent's claim that he reasonably anticipated that his greenhouse would not be subject to observation from that altitude."[101] Presently, use of UAVs in U.S. airspace is considerably less common. The FAA has issued only approximately 300 licenses for drone use in U.S. airspace.[102] The general public would likely find it exceedingly unusual for a drone to fly over their homes taking surveillance photographs. This rarity might factor into a reviewing court's determination of whether individuals have a legitimate expectation of privacy from various forms of drone surveillance while in a public place.[103]

The federal government's authority to use unmanned aircraft is undoubtedly at its maximum near U.S. borders. One of the federal government's only affirmative duties is to protect citizens from external harm.[104] This includes securing the borders. The Court has hesitated from interfering with the performance of this duty, and it would in all likelihood demonstrate the same deference when it comes to the use of UAVs. Moreover, the Supreme Court's rulings in border cases have all involved active searches—either a physical search of a vehicle or stopping and questioning a vehicle's passenger. Surveillance by UAVs, on the other hand, may be considered more passive and therefore may be even less likely to run afoul of Fourth Amendment requirements. Drone surveillance does not require any physical manipulation of a person or his things. UAVs also do not require the seizure of a person for any period of time (though drone surveillance may lead to law enforcement physically apprehending a person who is seen engaging in suspected illegal activity). However, the Court has shown some reticence about giving law enforcement carte blanche search power at the border. Roving vehicle patrols and indiscriminate searches in *Almeida-Sanchez v. United States* and *United States v. Brignoni-Ponce* were deemed unconstitutional.[105] It is unclear whether this reticence would extend to drone surveillance along the border if it were to become significantly widespread.

Technology Used

Like location, the technology used by UAVs may be a decisive factor considered by courts in determining whether individuals have a legitimate expectation of privacy in the object or area of the challenged drone search. Technological developments make it increasingly easy to share and acquire personal information about others, oftentimes without their direct knowledge or consent. As surveillance technology advances and becomes ever-present in Americans' lives, people's conception of privacy may tend to oscillate. Justice Scalia, writing for the majority in *Kyllo v. United States*, remarked on this trend:

> It would be foolish to contend that the degree of privacy secured to citizens by the Fourth Amendment has been entirely unaffected by the advance of technology. For example, ... the technology enabling human flight has exposed to public view (and hence, we have said, to official observation) uncovered portions of the house and its curtilage that once were private. The question we confront today is what limits there are upon this power of technology to shrink the realm of guaranteed privacy.[106]

Justice Alito, joined by three other Justices in his *United States v. Jones* concurrence, likewise observed:

> The *Katz* test rests on the assumption that this hypothetical reasonable person has a well-developed and stable set of privacy expectations. But technology can change those expectations. Dramatic technological change may lead to periods in which popular expectations are in flux and may ultimately produce significant changes in popular attitudes. New technology may provide increased convenience or security at the expense of privacy, and many people may find the tradeoff worthwhile. And even if the public does not

> welcome the diminution of privacy that new technology entails, they may eventually reconcile themselves to this development as inevitable.[107]

The crucial question, then, is whether drones have the potential to be significantly more invasive than traditional surveillance technologies such as manned aircraft or low-powered cameras— technologies that have been upheld in previous cases. In this vein, some have asked whether using sophisticated digital platforms on a drone is any different from attaching the same instrument to a lamppost or traditional aircraft.[108] Take, for example, the tracking of license plates. Currently, many states and municipalities employ automatic license plate readers (ALPRs), which are usually mounted on police vehicles or stationary objects along the streets, to take a snapshot of a license plate as a car drives by, and store this information in a large database for possible later use by law enforcement.[109] It is alleged that these devices can be used to track a person's movements when police aggregate the data from a multitude of ALPR stations.[110] A majority of the reviewing federal circuit courts have held that a person has no reasonable expectation of privacy in his license plate number.[111]

However, it appears that no federal court has addressed the constitutionality of the use of ALPRs (whether attached to a drone, manned vehicle, or a stationary device), as opposed to plate numbers collected by a human observer. Nonetheless, the question remains whether attaching an ALPR—or any similar sophisticated technology—to a drone would alter the constitutionality of its use by law enforcement. Some say yes, arguing that the sophistication of drone technology in and of itself "present[s] a unique threat to privacy."[112] Drones are smaller, can fly longer, and can be built more cheaply than traditional aircraft. For instance, defense firm Lockheed Martin's Stalker—a small, electrically powered drone—can be recharged from the ground using a laser.[113] It now has a flight time of more than 48 hours. As this technology advances, it is reported that some drones could theoretically "stay in the air forever."[114] Unlike a stationary license plate tracker or video camera, drones can lock on a target's every move for days, and possibly weeks and months. This ability to closely monitor an individual's movements with pinpoint accuracy may raise more significant constitutional concerns than some other types of surveillance technology.

Furthermore, the technology and sophistication of drones may mark a considerable departure from the traditional technologies used in the three manned aerial surveillance cases decided by the Supreme Court. First, all three holdings in *Ciraolo*, *Riley*, and *Dow Chemical* were premised on naked-eye searches. Chief Justice Burger remarked in *Dow Chemical*: "It may well be, as the government concedes, that surveillance of private property using highly sophisticated surveillance equipment not generally available to the public, such as satellite technology, might be constitutionally proscribed absent a warrant."[115] As noted above, the sophistication of surveillance technology available to drones, such as facial recognition or laser radar which can "see" through walls, may lead some to question the relevance of prior Fourth Amendment jurisprudence concerning more rudimentary forms of surveillance technology.

The sophistication of drones also has the ability to break down any practical privacy safeguard. In the pre-computer age, the greatest privacy protections were neither constitutional nor statutory, but practical. Putting officers everywhere in the community cost too much for local police departments. This acted as a natural barrier to excessive police presence. Drones are not hindered by similar limitations. This is similar to the expansion of GPS technology observed by the five concurring Justices in *United States v. Jones*. There, Justice Sotomayor, writing for herself, noted that because GPS technology was cheaper and performed in a surreptitious manner, it "evades the ordinary checks that constrain abusive law enforcement practices: limited police resources and community hostility."[116] Justice Alito sounded a similar note in *Jones*: "Traditional surveillance for any extended period of time was difficult and costly and therefore rarely undertaken. [GPS devices] make long-term monitoring relatively easy and cheap."[117] Instead of putting more officers in the field, a police force could put drones in the sky for potentially less expense. Already, drones with video capabilities can be purchased from private vendors for a few hundred dollars.[118] This access to inexpensive technology may significantly reduce budgetary concerns that once checked the government from widespread surveillance.

The duration and pervasiveness of drone surveillance—two factors closely associated with the technology employed by law enforcement—may also influence a court's Fourth Amendment analysis. Consider the Fifth Circuit Court of Appeals' ruling in *United States v. CuevasSanchez*.[119] In that case, federal law enforcement agents suspected the defendant was using his home as a drop house for drug traffickers. After obtaining a court order, the agents installed a video camera on a utility pole overlooking the defendant's 10-foot high fence surrounding his back yard. The officers observed the removal of drugs from the gas tanks of several cars parked in the defendant's yard. Based on these observations, the defendant was arrested whereupon the police seized a large amount of marijuana. At trial, the defendant moved to suppress the evidence on the basis that the warrant was defective. However, the court first addressed whether the video surveillance was a search under the Fourth Amendment. In determining that the video surveillance was a search, the panel noted that this "was not a one-time overhead flight or a glance over the fence by a passer-by.... It does not follow that *Ciraolo* authorizes any type of surveillance whatever just because one type of minimally-intrusive aerial observation is possible."[120] Drones have the capability to stay in the air for long periods of time and can hover in one location. Similar to the mounted camera in *Cuevas-Sanchez*, this permits law enforcement to employ drones in prolonged surveillance operations. This capability may sway a court's determination of whether certain types of warrantless drone surveillance are compatible with the Fourth Amendment.

Warrant Requirement and Suspicionless Drone Searches

Applying the Fourth Amendment to drones requires application of the threshold question: was there a search? Again, this will depend on all the factors discussed above—the area of the search, the technology used, and whether society would respect the target's expectation of privacy in the place searched. If a reviewing court concludes that the drone surveillance was not a search, neither a warrant nor any degree of individualized suspicion would be required. If, however, the court concluded there was a search, then a court would ask whether a warrant is required, if one of the exceptions apply, and what level of suspicion, if any, is necessary to uphold the search.

Unless a meaningful distinction can be made between drone surveillance and more traditional forms of government tracking, existing jurisprudence suggests that a reviewing court would likely uphold drone surveillance conducted with no individualized suspicion when conducted for purposes other than strict law enforcement. The Supreme Court has hesitated from interfering in what they see as the executive's function in protecting the health and safety of the American population. As Chief Justice Rehnquist noted in the *Sitz*, the Court does not want

> to transfer from politically accountable officials to the courts the decision as to which among reasonable alternative law enforcement techniques should be employed to deal with serious public danger.... [F]or purposes of Fourth Amendment analysis, the choice among

> such reasonable alternatives remains with the governmental officials who have a unique understanding of, and a responsibility for, limited public resources, including a finite number of police officers.[121]

The Court may defer to law enforcement officials in the drone context also. There are countless instances where the government may seek to utilize drones for health and safety purposes that go beyond mere law enforcement. These may include firefighting, search and rescue missions, traffic safety enforcement, or environmental protection. If, on other hand, surveillance is conducted primarily to enforce the law, a warrant may be required, unless one of the exceptions to the warrant requirement applies.

LEGISLATIVE PROPOSALS IN THE 113TH CONGRESS TO CONSTRAIN DOMESTIC USE OF DRONES

Although the Supreme Court is the final arbiter of the Constitution, Congress and the President can provide for greater regulation of drones than the Fourth Amendment requires. Congress has taken such steps over the years to address government surveillance of communications in transit (commonly known as wiretapping),[122] communications in storage such as e-mails,[123] bank records,[124] and health records,[125] among a host of other private information. Several measures have been introduced in the 113th Congress that would restrict the domestic use of drones, and establish arguably greater constraints on their usage than the Fourth Amendment requires. Several bills were prompted by a general concern for potential privacy intrusions by federal and state law enforcement and executive agencies.[126]

Preserving Freedom from Unwarranted Surveillance Act of 2013 (H.R. 972)

In the 113th Congress, Representative Austin Scott has introduced the Preserving Freedom from Unwarranted Surveillance Act of 2013 (H.R. 972).[127] This bill would require any entity acting under the authority of the federal government to obtain a warrant based upon probable cause before conducting drone surveillance to investigate violations of criminal law or regulations. There are, however, several exceptions to this warrant requirement: (1) to prevent or deter illegal entry of any persons or illegal substances into the United States; (2) when a law enforcement officer possesses reasonable suspicion that under particular circumstances "swift action to prevent imminent danger to life or serious damage to property, or to forestall the imminent escape of a suspect, or destruction of evidence" is necessary; or (3) when the Secretary of Homeland Security determines credible intelligence indicates a high risk of a terrorist attack by a specific individual or organization. H.R. 972 would create a right to sue for any violation of its prohibitions.

Preserving American Privacy Act of 2013 (H.R. 637)

Representative Ted Poe introduced the Preserving American Privacy Act of 2013 (H.R. 637), which would restrict the domestic use of drones.[128] To begin, the bill regulates surveillance of "covered information," which means "information that is reasonably likely to enable identification of an individual" or "information about an individual's property that is not in plain view." H.R. 637 would create a general prohibition on the use of drones to collect covered information or disclose covered information so collected. It does, however, provide the following exceptions:

- *Warrant*. Law enforcement obtains a court-issued warrant and serves a copy of the warrant on the target of the search within 10 days of the surveillance. However, notice need not be provided if it would jeopardize an ongoing criminal or national security investigation.
- *General Order*. Law enforcement obtains a court-issued order based upon "specific and articulable facts showing a reasonable suspicion of criminal activity and a reasonable probability" that the operation "will provide evidence of such criminal activity." The order may authorize surveillance in a stipulated public area for no more than 48 hours which may be renewed for a total of 30 days. Notice of the operation must be provided to the target no later than 10 days after the operation. Alternatively, notice may be provided not less than 48 hours before the operation in a major publication, on a government website, or with signs posted in the area of the operation.
- *Border searches*. Operation is within 25 miles of national border.
- *Consent*. The targeted individual has provided prior written consent.
- *Emergencies*. Emergency situation involves danger of death or serious physical injury, conspiratorial activities threatening the national

security interest, or conspiratorial activities characteristic of organized crime, where a warrant cannot be obtained with due diligence. Law enforcement must then obtain a warrant within 48 hours of such operation.

Any evidence obtained in violation of this act is not admissible in any trial or adjudicative proceeding. Additionally, H.R. 637 requires any governmental entity applying for a certificate or license to operate a UAS to also file a data collection statement with the Attorney General. The statement must include the following:

- Purpose for which the UAS will be used
- Whether the UAS is capable of collecting covered information
- The length of time the information will be retained
- A point of contact for citizen feedback
- The particular unit of governmental entity responsible for safe and appropriate operation of the UAS
- The rank and title of the individual who may authorize the operation of the UAS
- The applicable data minimization policies barring the collection of covered information unrelated to the investigation of crime and requiring the destruction of covered information that is no longer relevant to the investigation of a crime
- Applicable audit and oversight procedures.

Under H.R. 637, the Attorney General may request that the Secretary of Transportation revoke the license or certificate of any entity that fails to file a data collection statement. Further, H.R. 637 contains a provision permitting administrative discipline against an officer who intentionally violates a provision of this act.

Drone Aircraft Privacy and Transparency Act of 2013 (H.R. 1262)

Representative Ed Markey introduced the Drone Aircraft Privacy and Transparency Act of 2013 (H.R. 1262).[129] This bill would amend the FAA Modernization and Reform Act of 2012 to create a comprehensive scheme to regulate government actors' use of drones, including data collection requirements and enforcement mechanisms.

First, this bill would require the Secretary of Transportation, with input from the Secretary of Commerce, the Chairman of the Federal Trade Commission, and the Chief Privacy Officer of the Department of Homeland Security, to study any potential threats to privacy protections posed by the introduction of drones in the national airspace. Next, the bill would prohibit the FAA from issuing a license to operate a drone unless the application for such use included a "data collection statement." This statement would require the following items:

- A list of individuals who would have the authority to operate the drone
- The location in which the drone will be used
- The maximum period it will be used
- Whether the drone would be collecting information about individuals

If the drone will be used to collect personal information, the statement must include the following:

- The circumstances in which such information will be used
- The kinds of information collected and the conclusions drawn from it
- The type of data minimization procedures to be employed
- Whether the information will be sold, and if so, under what circumstances
- How long the information would be stored
- Procedures for destroying irrelevant data.

The statement must also include information about the possible impact on privacy protections posed by the operation under that license and steps to be taken to mitigate this impact. Additionally, the statement must include the contact information of the drone operator; a process for determining what information has been collected about an individual; and a process for challenging the accuracy of such data. Finally, the FAA would be required to post the data collection statement on the Internet.

In addition to the data collection statement, any law enforcement agency which operates a drone must file with the FAA a "data minimization statement." This statement must include policies adopted by the agency that

- minimize the collection of information and data unrelated to the investigation of a crime under a warrant,
- require the destruction of data that is no longer relevant to the investigation of a crime,
- establish procedures for the method of such destruction, and
- establish oversight and audit procedures to ensure the agency operates a UAS in accordance with the data collection statement filed with the FAA.

H.R. 1262 includes several enforcement mechanisms. First, the FAA may revoke a license of a user that does not comply with these requirements. The Federal Trade Commission would have the primary authority to enforce the data collection requirements just stated. Additionally, the Attorney General of each state, or an official or agency of a state, is empowered to file a civil suit if there is reason to believe that the privacy interests of residents of that state have been threatened or adversely affected. H.R. 1262 would also create a private right of action for a person injured by a violation of this legislation.

CONCLUSION

The introduction of drones into American airspace raises many legal and policy questions. For instance, how far can the government go in its attempts to maintain security and ensure that laws are enforced? What level of privacy should Americans expect in an age where technology facilitating the acquisition of personal information expands at a phenomenal pace? Currently, there is a vast body of Fourth Amendment law that governs the circumstances in which law enforcement must obtain a warrant before conducting surveillance.

However, the sheer sophistication of drone technology and the sensors they can carry may remove drones from this traditional Fourth Amendment framework. Beyond the courts and the Constitution, what role should Congress and the President play in regulating the introduction of drones inside the United States? As the integration of drones for domestic surveillance operations quickly accelerates, these questions and others will be posed to the American people and their political leaders.

End Notes

[1] The term "domestic drone surveillance" as used in this report is designed to cover a wide range of government uses including, but not limited to, investigating and deterring criminal or regulatory violations; conducting health and safety inspections; performing search and rescue missions; patrolling the national borders; and conducting environmental investigations.

[2] Letter from Representatives Edward J. Markey and Joe Barton, Co-Chairmen of the Congressional Bi-Partisan Privacy Caucus, to Michael P. Huerta, Acting Administrator of the Federal Aviation Administration (April 19, 2012) ("[I]n addition to benefits, there is also the potential for drone technology to enable invasive and pervasive surveillance without adequate privacy protections."), *available at* http://markey.house.gov/sites/markey.house.gov/files/documents/ 4-19-12.Letter%20FAA%20Drones%20.pdf; AMERICAN CIVIL LIBERTIES UNION, PROTECTING PRIVACY FROM AERIAL SURVEILLANCE: RECOMMENDATIONS FOR GOVERNMENT USE OF DRONE AIRCRAFT 1 (2011), *available at* https://www.aclu.org/files/assets

[3] Mark Brunswick, *Spies in the sky signal new age of surveillance*, STARTRIBUNE (July 22, 2012, 6:26 a.m.), *available at* http://www.startribune.com/local/163304886.html?refer=y.

[4] Some state and local officials have expressed interest in employment of drones for public safety and law enforcement purposes. *See, e.g.*, Brianne Carter, *Gov. Bob McDonnell supports drones policing Virginia*, ABC NEWS (May 30, 2012), *available at* http://www.wjla.com/articles/2012/05/gov-bob-mcdonnell-supports-drones-policing-virginia76464.html; *Unmanned Aircraft Systems Within the Homeland: Security Game Changer? Hearing Before the Subcomm. on Oversight, Investigations, and Management of the H. Comm. on Homeland Sec.*, 112th Cong. 3 (2012) (statement of William R. McDaniel, Chief Deputy, Montgomery County Sheriff's Office, Conroe, TX) ("UAV systems for public safety agencies are extremely viable, effective, and economical means to enhance the public safety response to critical incidents.").

[5] The Supreme Court remarked in *Kyllo v. United States*, 533 U.S. 27, 37 (2001):

> The ability to 'see' through walls and other opaque barriers is a clear, and scientifically feasible, goal of law enforcement research and development. The National Law Enforcement and Corrections Technology Center, a program within the United States Department of Justice, features on its Internet Website projects that include a 'Radar-Based Through-the-Wall Surveillance System,' 'Handheld Ultrasound Through the Wall Surveillance,' and a 'Radar Flashlight' that 'will enable law officers to detect individuals through interior building walls.'

[6] *U.S. Supports Some Domestic Drone Use, But Public Registers Concern About Own Privacy* 1, Monmouth University Polling Institute (June 12, 2012), *available at* http://www.monmouth.edu.

[7] U.S. CONST. amend IV.

[8] Cooper v. Aaron, 358 U.S. 1, 18 (1958) ("[Marbury v. Madison] declared the basic principle that the federal judiciary is supreme in the exposition of the law of the Constitution, and that principle has ever since been respected by this Court and the Country as a permanent and indispensable feature of our constitutional system.").

[9] In reaction to the Supreme Court's ruling in *United States v. Miller*, 425 U.S. 435 (1976), that the privacy of an individual's bank records were generally not protected by the Fourth Amendment, Congress enacted the Right to Financial Privacy Act, P.L. 95-630, 92 Stat. 3697 (codified at 12 U.S.C. §3401-3422), creating a statutory protection for such records.

[10] DEP'T OF DEFENSE, DICTIONARY OF MILITARY AND ASSOCIATED TERMS 331 (2012). Unless expressly mentioned, the terms "unmanned aerial vehicle," "UAV," "unmanned aircraft system," "UAS," and "drone" are used interchangeably in this report.

[11] *Id.*

[12] See CRS Report R42136, *U.S. Unmanned Aerial Systems*, by Jeremiah Gertler, for a description of the various types of drones currently operated in the United States.

[13] FEDERAL AVIATION ADMINISTRATION, FAA AEROSPACE FORECAST: FISCAL YEARS 2010-2030, at 48 (2010), *available at* http://www.faa.gov/data_research/aviation /aerospace. The FAA has noted that "Federal agencies are planning to increase their use of UAS's. State and local governments envision using UAS's to aid in law enforcement and firefighting. Potential commercial uses are also possible, for example, in real estate photography or pipeline inspection. UAS's could perform some manned aircraft missions with less noise and fewer emissions." *Id.*

[14] *See, e.g.*, Intelligence Reform and Terrorism Prevention Act of 2004, P.L. 108-458, §5102, 118 Stat. 3638, 3732 (requesting that DHS test the feasibility of using unmanned aircraft to patrol the northern border of the United States).

[15] FAA Modernization and Reform Act of 2012, P.L. 112-95, §332, 126 Stat. 11, 73.

[16] *See* CRS Report RS21698, *Homeland Security: Unmanned Aerial Vehicles and Border Surveillance*, by Chad C. Haddal and Jeremiah Gertler.

[17] The OAM mission is to "protect the American people and the Nation's critical infrastructure through the coordinated use of integrated air and marine forces." DEP'T OF HOMELAND SECURITY, OFFICE OF INSPECTOR GENERAL, CBP'S USE OF UNMANNED AIRCRAFT SYSTEMS IN THE NATION'S BORDER SECURITY 2 (2012). These forces are used to "detect, interdict, and prevent acts of terrorism and the unlawful movement of people, illegal drugs, and other contraband toward or across U.S. borders." *Id.*

[18] There are over 300 total, including those issued to the following entities: City of Herrington, KS; Cornell University; Department of Energy Idaho National Laboratory; Eastern Gateway College Community College—Steubenville, OH; Miami-Dade Police Department; Mississippi Department of Marine Resources; North Little Rock Police Department, AR; Ogden Police Department, UT; Ohio University; Seattle Police Department; Texas A&M—Texas Engineering Experiment Station; Texas Department of Public Safety; Texas State University; University of Connecticut; University of Florida; U.S. Department of Agriculture Agricultural Research Service; Utah State University; Virginia Tech. *See* Unmanned Aircraft Systems, Federal Aviation Administration, http://www.faa.gov /about/initiatives/uas/.

[19] *New age of surveillance*, *supra* note 3.

[20] Brian Bennett, *Drones Tested as Tools for Police and Firefighters*, LOS ANGELES TIMES (August 5, 2012 5:00 A.M.), http://www.latimes.com/news/nationworld/nation/la-na-drones-testing

[21] The U.S. Army recently acquired a 1.8 gigapixel camera for use on its drones. This camera offers 900 times the pixels of a 2 megapixel camera found in some cell phones. It can track objects on the ground 65 miles away from an altitude of 20,000 feet. *US Army unveils 1.8 gigapixel camera helicopter drone*, BBC NEWS (December 29, 2011 6:11 p.m.), http://www.bbc.com/news/technology

[22] Infrared cameras, also known as thermal imaging, can see objects through walls based on the relative levels of heat produced by the objects. *See* Draganflyer X6, Thermal Infrared Camera, http://www.draganfly.com/uav-helicopter/ draganflyer-x6/features/flir-camera.php.

[23] This sensor can recognize and permit drones to track vehicles based on license plate numbers. Customs and Border Protection Today, Unmanned Aerial Vehicles Support Border Security (July 2004), http://www.cbp.gov/xp/ CustomsToday/2004/Aug/other/aerial_vehicles.xml.

[24] This sensor produces three-dimensional images, and has the capability to see through trees and foliage. U.S. ARMY, UAS CENTER FOR EXCELLENCE, "EYES OF THE ARMY" US ARMY ROADMAP FOR UNMANNED AIRCRAFT SYSTEMS 2010- 2035, at 83 (2010).

[25] *See* Clay Dillow, *Army Developing Drones that Can Recognize Your Face from a Distance*, POPSCI (September 28, 2011), 5:01 p.m.), *available at* http://www.popsci.com/technology /article/2011-09/army-wants-drones-can-recognizeyour-face-and-read-your-mind.

[26] U.S. CONST. amend IV.

[27] Olmstead v. United States, 277 U.S. 438, 466 (1928).

[28] *Id.*

[29] Katz v. United States, 389 U.S. 347, 351 (1967).

[30] *Id.* at 359.

[31] *Id.* at 351.

[32] *Id.* at 361 (Harlan, J., concurring).

[33] *Id.* at 351.

[34] *Id.* at 361 (Harlan, J., concurring); *see also* Oliver v. United States, 466 U.S. 170 (1984).

> We have frequently acknowledged that privacy interests are not coterminous with property rights. E. g., United States v. Salvucci, 448 U.S. 83, 91 (1980). However, because "property rights reflect society's explicit recognition of a person's authority to act as he wishes in certain areas, [they] should be considered in determining whether an individual's expectations of privacy are reasonable." Rakas v. Illinois, 439 U.S. 128, 153 (1978) (Powell, J., concurring). Indeed, the Court has suggested that, insofar as "[one] of the main rights attaching to property is the right to exclude others, ... one who owns or lawfully possesses or controls property will in all likelihood have a legitimate expectation of privacy by virtue of this right to exclude." *Id.*, at 144, n. 12.

Oliver, 466 U.S. at 189-90.

[35] United States v. Jones, 132 S. Ct. 945, 950 n.3 (2012).

[36] *Id.*

[37] DANIEL SOLOVE, UNDERSTANDING PRIVACY 59 (2008).

[38] U.S. CONST. amend IV.

[39] Silverman v. United States, 365 U.S. 505, 512 (1961) ("At the very core stands the right of a man to retreat into his own home and be free from unreasonable government intrusion.").

[40] United States v. Watson, 423 U.S. 411 (1976).

[41] Payton v. New York, 445 U.S. 573, 603 (1980). This protection not only covers traditional houses, but apartments, Clinton v. Virginia, 377 U.S 158 (1963), and motel rooms, Stoner v. California, 376 U.S. 483 (1964).

[42] Kyllo v. United States, 533 U.S. 27, 29-30 (2001).

[43] *Id.* at 31.

[44] *Id.* at 34.

[45] In one case, police observation of marijuana plants through a crack in the house's siding did not constitute an unlawful search. *United States v. Hammett*, 236 F.3d 1054, 1061 (9th Cir. 2001). In another, the court held that the police officer's observation of contraband through the front dining room window was not unlawful. *United States v. Taylor*, 90 F.3d 903, 909 (4th Cir. 1996).

[46] Coolidge v. New Hampshire, 403 U.S. 443, 466 (1971).

[47] United States v. Hester, 365 U.S 57 (1924) (distinguishing between the doctrines of curtilage and open fields).

[48] The Court has defined curtilage as "the area to which extends the intimate activity associated with the 'sanctity of a man's home and the privacies of life.'" Oliver v. United States, 466 U.S. 170, 180 (1984) (quoting Boyd v. United States, 116 U.S. 616, 630 (1886)).

[49] United States v. Dunn, 480 U.S. 294, 301 (1987).

[50] California v. Ciraolo, 476 U.S. 207, 213 (1986).

[51] Dow Chemical Co. v. United States, 476 U.S. 227, 234-35 (1986) (quoting *Oliver*, 466 U.S. at 179).

[52] Maisano v. Welcher, 940 F.2d 499 (9th Cir. 1991).

[53] *Ciraolo*, 476 U.S. at 213.

[54] *Id.* at 207.

[55] *Id.* at 213.

[56] *Id.* at 213-214. It should be noted that although the police did take photographs with a 35-millimeter camera, the warrant relied on naked-eye observations and not the photographs. Thus, the holding was based on the naked-eye observations, unaided by the camera.

[57] *Id.* at 213 (citing 49 U.S.C. §1304).

[58] Florida v. Riley, 488 U.S. 445, 448 (1989).

[59] *Id.*

[60] *Dow Chemical Co.*, 476 U.S. 227.

[61] *Id.* at 239

[62] United States v. Knotts, 460 U.S. 276 (1983); United States v. Karo, 468 U.S. 705 (1984).

[63] *Knotts*, 460 U.S. at 279. The Court reiterated that its analysis was based on the fact that the beeper was tracked within the vicinity of a home, not actually in the home. *Id*

[64] *Karo*, 468 U.S. at 714.

[65] *Id.* at 715.

[66] United States v. Jones, 132 S. Ct. 945 (2012).

[67] *Id.* at 949. *See generally* CRS Report R42511, *United States v. Jones: GPS Monitoring, Property, and Privacy*, by Richard M. Thompson II.

[68] *Jones*, 132 S. Ct. at 955 (Sotomayor, J., concurring).

[69] *Id.*

[70] Although the two concurring opinions in *Jones* arguably do not constitute binding precedent, lower courts have combined them as a possible alternative holding. *See* United States v. Hanna, No. 11-20678-CR, 2012 WL 279435, at *3 (S.D. Fla. Jan. 3, 2012) (analyzing the issue of Fourth Amendment standing to contest GPS surveillance under both the trespass theory and *Katz*'s privacy test); State v. Zahn, No. 25584, 2012 WL 862707 (S.D. Mar. 14, 2012) (holding that both the trespass approach and the mosaic theory can apply to GPS tracking); *but see* United States v. Bradshaw, No. 1:11-CR-257, 2012 WL 774964 (N.D. Ohio Mar. 8, 2012) (noting that the *Jones* majority did not adopt the mosaic theory).

[71] 8 U.S.C. 1357.

[72] 19 U.S.C. §482. In the 112th Congress, the House of Representatives introduced H.R. 1505, which would enlarge CBP's authority to secure U.S. borders on federal land. H.R. 1505; *see also* John S. Adams, *Border bill would expand Homeland Security powers*, USA TODAY (September 26, 2011).

[73] United States v. Flores-Montano, 541 U.S. 149, 152 (2004).

[74] Cady v. Dombrowski, 413 U.S. 433, 439 (1973).

[75] United States v. Montoya De Hernandez, 473 U.S. 531, 538 (1985).

[76] *Id.*

[77] United States v. Beras, 183 F.3d 22, 24 (1st Cir. 1999) (ruling that pat down of defendant's legs was routine search).

[78] United States v. Kelly, 302 F.3d 291, 294-95 (5th Cir. 2002).

[79] United States v. Okafor, 285 F.3d 842 (9th Cir. 2002).

[80] *Montoya De Hernandez*, 473 U.S. at 541.

[81] *Id.*

[82] United States v. Asbury, 586 F.2d 973, 975 (1978).

[83] United States v. Ogberaha, 771 F.2d 655, 657 (2d Cir. 1985).

[84] Almeida-Sanchez v. United States, 413 U.S. 266, 267-68 (1973).

[85] *Id.* at 272-73 ("For example, searches at an established station near the border, at a point marking the confluence of two or more roads that extend from the border, might be functional equivalents from border searches. For another example, a search of the passengers and cargo of an airplane arriving at a St. Louis airport after a nonstop flight from Mexico would clearly be the functional equivalent of a border search."). Like *Almeida-Sanchez*, Border Patrol agents in *United States v. Brignoni-Ponce* stopped an individual's vehicle as part of a roving patrol solely because the occupants appeared to be of Mexican descent, with no proof of illegal activity. *United States v. Brignoni-Ponce*, 422 U.S. 873, 874-75 (1975). Again, the Court struck down this practice of suspicionless stops, remarking that "[i]n the context of border area stops, the reasonableness requirement of the Fourth Amendment demands something more than the broad and unlimited discretion sought by the Government. Roads near the border carry not only aliens seeking to enter the country illegally, but a large volume of legitimate traffic as well." *Id.* at 882.

[86] Mincey v. Arizona, 437 U.S. 385, 390 (1978) (citation omitted).

[87] Johnson v. Untied States, 333 U.S. 10, 14 (1948) ("The right of officers to thrust themselves into a home is also a grave concern, not only to the individual but to a society which chooses to dwell in reasonable security and freedom from surveillance. When the right of privacy must reasonably yield to the right of search is, as a rule, to be decided by a judicial officer, not by a policeman or government enforcement agent."). Probable cause is found when, looking at the "totality-of-the-circumstances" there "is a fair probability that contraband or evidence of a crime will be found in a particular place." Illinois v. Gates, 462 U.S. 213, 238 (1983).

[88] Eve Brensike Primus, *Disentangling Administrative Searches*, 111 COLUM. L. REV. 254, 256 (2011).

[89] Nat'l Treasury Employees Union v. Von Raab, 489 U.S. 656, 665-66 (1989).

[90] Primus, *supra* note 88, at 263.

[91] United States v. Martinez-Fuerte, 428 U.S. 543, 566 (1976).

[92] United States v. Biswell, 406 U.S 311, 317 (inspection of gun dealer's storeroom) ("We have little difficulty in concluding that where, as here, regulatory inspections further urgent federal interest, and the possibilities of abuse and the threat to privacy are not of impressive dimensions, the inspection may proceed without a warrant where specifically authorized by statute.").

[93] Mich. Dep't of State Police v. Sitz, 496 U.S. 444, 455 (1990).

[94] *Id.* at 455.

[95] City of Indianapolis v. Edmund, 531 U.S. 32 (2000).

[96] *Id.* at 42.

[97] *Id.*

[98] EYES OF THE ARMY, *supra* note 24.

[99] *See generally,* Paul McBride, *Beyond Orwell: The Application of Unmanned Aircraft Systems in Domestic Surveillance Operations*, 74 J. Air. L. & Com. 627, 655-56 ("This implies that although the curtilage does not benefit from the absolute protection afforded to the interior of the home, there is a close relationship between the two, and that technology directed at the home and its curtilage will be subjected to a more skeptical analysis than would be applied in a case involving open fields or industrial areas.").

[100] California v. Ciraolo, 476 U.S. 207, 215 (1986).

[101] Florida v. Riley, 488 U.S. 445, 451-52 (1989).

[102] Federal Aviation Administration, *supra* note 18.

[103] *Ciraolo*, 476 U.S. at 212. However, in determining society's privacy expectations, a reviewing court might also take into consideration the proliferation of aerial mapping such as Google Maps and Google Earth conducted by private actors. *See generally* Google Maps, Street View, http://www.google

[104] U.S. CONST. art. IV, §4 ("The United States shall guarantee to every State in this Union a Republican Form of Government, and shall protect each of them against Invasion[.]").

[105] Almeida-Sanchez v. United States, 413 U.S. 266 (1973); United States v. Brignoni-Ponce, 422 U.S. 873 (1975).

[106] Kyllo v. United States, 533 U.S. 27, 33-34 (2001).

[107] United States v. Jones, 132 S. Ct. 945, 962 (2012) (Alito, J., concurring).

[108] Stanford Law Review Symposium, *Drones—Privacy Paradox: Privacy and its Conflicting Values* (February 2, 2012), http://cyberlaw.stanford.edu/multimedia

[109] *ACLU Seeks Details on Automatic License Plate Readers in Massive Nationwide Request,* AMERICAN CIVIL LIBERTIES UNION (July 31, 2012), http://www.aclu.org/technology-

[110] *Id.*

[111] *See, e.g.*, Olabisiomotosho v. City of Houston, 185 F.3d 521, 529 (5th Cir. 1999) ("A motorist has no privacy interest in her license plate number. Like the area outside the cartilage [sic] of a dwelling, a car's license plate number is constantly open to the plain view of passersby.") (internal citation and quotation marks omitted); United States v. Ellison, 462 F.3d 557, 562 (6th Cir. 2006) ("No argument can be made that a motorist seeks to keep the information on his license plate private. The very purpose of a license plate number, like that of a Vehicle Identification Number, is to provide identifying information to law enforcement officials and others."); United States v. Castaneda, 494 F.3d 1146, 1151 (9th Cir. 2007); United States v. Walraven, 892 F.2d 972, 974 (10th 1989).

[112] *Using Unmanned Aircraft Systems Within the Homeland: Security Game Changer? Hearing Before the Subcomm. on Oversight, Investigations, and Management of the H. Comm. on Homeland Sec.*, 112th Cong. 3 (2012) (statement of Amie Stepanovich, Counsel, Electronic Privacy Information Center).

[113] Mark Brown, *Lockheed uses ground-based laser to recharge drone mid-flight*, WIRED (July 12, 2012), *available at* http://www.wired.co.uk/news/archive/2012-07/12/lockheed-lasers

[114] *Id.* Lockheed has reportedly been working on extending flight times from days to months. *Id.*

[115] *Dow Chemical*, 476 U.S. at 238.

[116] United States v. Jones, 132 S. Ct. 945, 956 (Sotomayor, J., concurring) (internal quotation marks omitted).

[117] *Id.*

[118] *See, e.g.,* Apple Store, Parrot AR.Drone 2.0, http://store.apple.com/us/product/H8859ZM/A /parrot-ar-drone-2-0. This aircraft, is remote-controlled by an iPhone or iPad, and has a high-definition camera that can take both pictures and videos. *Id.*

[119] United States v. Cuevas-Sanchez, 821 F.2d 248 (5th Cir. 1987).

[120] *Id.* at 251.

[121] Mich. Dep't of State Police v. Sitz, 496 U.S. 444, 453-54 (1990).

[122] Omnibus Crime Control and Safe Streets Act of 1968, P.L. 90-351, 87 Stat. 197, 211 (codified at 18 U.S.C. §2510- 2522).

[123] Electronic Communications Privacy Act of 1986, P.L. 99-508, 100 Stat. 1848 (codified at 18 U.S.C. §2701-2712).

[124] Right to Financial Privacy Act, P.L. 95-630, 92 Stat. 3697 (codified at 12 U.S.C. §3401-3422).

[125] Health Insurance Portability and Accountability Act of 1996, P.L. 104-191, 110 Stat. 1936.

[126] Several bills introduced in the 113th Congress aim to restrict the government's use of drones to lethally target U.S. citizens on U.S. soil. See, e.g., No Armed Drones Act of 2013, H.R. 1083, 113th Cong (1st Sess. 2013); S. 505, 113th Cong. (1st Sess. 2013). These bills, however, are beyond the scope of this report.

[127] H.R. 972, 113th Cong. (1st Sess. 2013). Senator Rand Paul filed similar legislation in the 112th Congress, but has not re-introduced it in the 113th Congress. *See* S. 3287, 112th Cong. (2d Sess. 2012). Unlike H.R. 972, S. 3287 included an express exclusionary rule for evidence obtained in violation of the act.

[128] H.R. 637, 113th Cong. (1st Sess. 2013).

[129] H.R. 1262, 113th Cong. (2d Sess. 2013).

INDEX

F

G

H

I

J

P

Q

R

S

T

U

V

W

Y